City Museums and
City Development

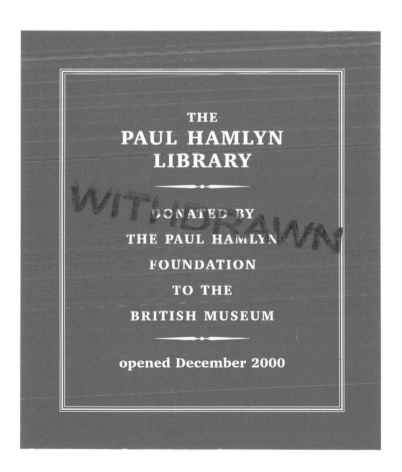

City Museums and
City Development

EDITED BY IAN JONES, ROBERT R.
MACDONALD, AND DARRYL McINTYRE

ALTAMIRA
PRESS

A Division of
ROWMAN & LITTLEFIELD PUBLISHERS, INC.
Lanham • New York • Toronto • Plymouth, UK

ALTAMIRA PRESS
A division of Rowman & Littlefield Publishers, Inc.
A wholly owned subsidary of The Rowman & Littlefield Publishing Group, Inc.
4501 Forbes Boulevard, Suite 200, Lanham, MD 20706
www.altamirapress.com

Estover Road, Plymouth PL6 7PY, United Kingdom

British Library Cataloguing in Publication Information Available

Library of Congress Cataloging-in-Publication Data
City museums and city development / edited by Ian Jones, Robert R. Macdonald, and
Darryl McIntyre.
   p. cm.
  Based on papers from a conference held Aug. 2007 in Vienna, sponsored by
CAMOC, the Collections and Activities of Museums of Cities.
  Includes bibliographical references and index.
  ISBN-13: 978-0-7591-1180-6 (cloth : alk. paper)
  ISBN-10: 0-7591-1180-4 (cloth : alk. paper)
  ISBN-13: 978-0-7591-1232-2 (electronic)
  ISBN-10: 0-7591-1232-0 (electronic)
  1. Museums—Social aspects—Congresses. 2. Historical museums—Congresses. 3.
Cities and towns—Congresses. 4. City planning—Congresses. 5. Urban
renewal—Congresses. I. Jones, Ian, 1935- II. Macdonald, Robert R. III. McIntyre,
Darryl, 1949-

AM7.C565 2008
069—dc22

         069   JON

           2008020766

Printed in the United States of America

♾™ The paper used in this publication meets the minimum requirements of
American National Standard for Information Sciences—Permanence of Paper
for Printed Library Materials, ANSI/NISO Z39.48-1992.

Contents

Acknowledgments

Cities are where half of us now live: megacities like Mexico City (population nineteen million) or Tokyo, the biggest of them all (thirty-five million); relatively small cities, by contemporary standards, like Grenoble or Palermo, Norilsk or Curitiba; or really small places known only to a few, but which are important local centers. The statistics on cities pour out from books and from the reports of bodies like UN-HABITAT: Paris was one of the largest cities in the world in 1950—now it is out of the top twenty; São Paulo was not even in the top twenty in 1950—it's now in the top five; Moscow has doubled in size since the Second World War; Lagos grows at a rate of more than 5 percent a year; there are more people living in slum conditions in Mumbai than the total population of Nairobi; by 2030 there will be five billion people living in cities. Reading the reports of UN-HABITAT is a pretty sobering experience. We could have filled this book with all sorts of statistics about cities and city living. But statistics are the skeleton of the real thing—the flesh-and-blood city—and this book is about the ways a new generation of museums aims to understand this extraordinary artifact.

The book would not have been possible without the contribution of my fellow editors—Robert R. Macdonald, director emeritus of the Museum of the City of New York and vice chair of CAMOC (the International Council of Museums international committee for museums of cities, set up in Moscow in 2005), and Darryl McIntyre, group director, Public Programs at the Museum of London and a founding member of CAMOC—all our colleagues in CAMOC, and the staff of ICOM in Paris, who have done so much for our committee through their practical help and advice. It would also not have been possible without the unfailing support and guidance of Serena Leigh Krombach, the AltaMira Press acquisitions editor for museum studies and public history; Alden Perkins, the helpful and sympathetic production editor; and Marissa N. Marro, AltaMira's meticulous editorial assistant. Their professionalism has been impressive.

Then there is our chair, Galina Vedernikova, director general of Moscow City Museum and its branches, whose drive and determination made CAMOC possible.

Ian Jones
March 2008

1

Cities and Museums about Them

IAN JONES

Cities are the defining artifacts of civilization. All the achievements and failings of humanity are here. Civic buildings, monuments, archives and institutions are the touchstones by which our cultural heritage is passed from one generation to the next. We shape the city, then it shapes us.

John Reader[1]

Our history is to a substantial degree the description of the triumph of cities and city life.

J. John Palen[2]

It is in the city, this ancient confluence of the sacred, safe, and busy, where humanity's future will be shaped for centuries to come.

Joel Kotkin[3]

The theme of this book is the contribution a museum about a city can make to its development. The book owes its origins to a conference held in Vienna in August 2007 by the Collections and Activities of Museums of Cities (CAMOC), an international committee forming an integral part of the International Council of Museums, a partner organization of UNESCO based in Paris. The chapter on globalization by Georges Prévélakis provides the contemporary context within which the city museum has to operate; the chapters that follow reflect differing approaches to bearing witness to the city.

But why should we have a museum about a city? The short answer is— why not? In 1800 just 2 percent of the world's population were urban dwellers. By 2007, for the first time in human history, half of us were living in cities: the world had finally become urban.[4] Not only that, cities, as Georges Prévélakis points out in this book, are back on center stage after centuries in the wings. London, New York, Frankfurt, and Tokyo are financial centers that leap national boundaries; some cities are wealthier than whole countries and many, through migration, have a remarkably diverse, multicultural population. Many have real economic, cultural, and political power; in effect, they are city-states. It would be distinctly odd, therefore, if we did *not* have museums about these artifacts, which is what they are.

The scale and rapidity of urban development has been extraordinary. London in 1910 was seven times larger than it was in 1800—but Dhaka, Kinshasa, and Lagos are now forty times larger than they were in 1950, and China added more people to its cities in the 1980s than Europe (including Russia) did in the whole of the nineteenth century.[5] In Shanghai over five thousand buildings over eight stories have been built within twenty-five years.[6] In 2005 there were twenty megacities, that is, cities with a population of ten million or more (although across the world smaller cities and towns will continue to absorb most of the urban population).[7] Currently, 36.5 percent of Uruguayans live in Montevideo, 32.4 percent of Argentineans in Buenos Aires, 25 percent of the Irish in Dublin. Why not? That's where the jobs are, and the bright lights and where things happen and where the power is—or perhaps simply that's where people were born and where they have no option but to stay. In Belgium, 97.2 percent of the people live in urban areas.[8] The Netherlands, Brazil, Australia, Chile—all are overwhelmingly urban. And so it goes on, relentlessly and, seemingly, endlessly.

As cities grow, they produce slums. Even in the twenty-first century, city people can still live in conditions not very different from those of the great

FIGURE 1.1
The Casa da Marquesa de Santos. The mansion has been preserved as one of the few remaining examples of eighteenth-century architecture in São Paulo, a megacity of skyscrapers and favelas, wealth and poverty. The restoration of the building and its use as a new museum of the city is part of the rehabilitation program that aims to promote economic and social development in the historic center of the city, which, as in so many cities worldwide, has seen a population decline. © Ana Aparecida Villanueva Rodrigues.

industrial cities of the early nineteenth century. In fact, today's slums are larger—the population of Rio de Janeiro's slums, for example, is nearly the same as the total population of Helsinki, Finland's capital.[9]

Cities across the world are getting to resemble each other. They are becoming less different, less quirky, less odd, more banal, more homogenized.[10] The brands you can buy in Moscow you can buy in Tokyo or London or New York or Bangkok. We now go from one city to the other with speed and ease, and we take our tastes and habits with us, impregnating cities on the way. Global star architects design buildings that often have limited respect for local context. (Nothing new there, perhaps—after all, Athens and Rome have left their architectural mark everywhere.)

Then there are universal city phenomena such as congestion and pollution and the repopulation of city centers by young, affluent people, and the
middle-class flight to the suburbs—which in turn become growth points
and produce their own suburbs. It happens in London and Moscow; it happens in Rio de Janeiro and São Paulo. Gated communities, isolated from
the rest of city life by physical barriers, are common in the wealthier areas
of cities, reflecting perceived urban insecurity. You find them in London;
you find them in Mexico City.

A string of shortcomings, then, to city living. On the other hand, where
would we be without cities? Whatever their frequently dreadful problems,
cities shape the history of their countries and the world. People move to
them because they have hope. They can be exciting places, good to live in
and to work in. They can be beautiful; they can be works of collective ge-
nius like Paris or New York; they can also be ugly, noisy, and dirty—but
without them we would have nowhere to focus our energies, and without
cities, without large concentrations of people, there would be no empti-
ness, no wilderness, no countryside. Cities matter. They have a present and
a future; they are reinventing themselves in the postindustrial age—think
of the transformation of Bilbao as a "city of knowledge"—but they also
have a past, which is why we have had museums about them for many generations.

How do museums about this vast and extraordinary artifact make sense
of it all? How have they responded to the dramatic urbanization of the
world?

Across Europe, and indeed across much of the developed world, city
museums have been guardians of city treasures. Many are in grand buildings of the nineteenth century, reflecting city pride; full of paintings, sculpture, and silverware; showing off the taste of an elite or perhaps the taste of
a wealthy local industrialist. They illuminate the city's finest hours and the
high points of its history. Essentially they are eclectic museums of city history and the collecting habits of individuals. They avoid if possible the recent past and certainly the present. The best are admirable in their own
right and are always worth visiting, not least because they can surprise us
with the unexpected.

FIGURE 1.2
The proposed new home of Moscow City Museum. This redundant army depot in central Moscow, a few meters from a metro station (ideal for a city museum), is a fine example of nineteenth-century Moscow architecture. The conversion of the building complex will need a sensitive architectural solution in a city that has lost much of its great heritage over the years. © Moscow City Museum.

Yet, change has been in the air—a gradual change, but change nevertheless: The city museum is increasingly focusing on the city itself. The city has become the artifact. The past is now examined more critically and is frequently used to shed light on the present. Awkward, sensitive subjects like immigration or crime or the destruction of the built environment are tackled more often. The contemporary is seen as worthy of record and debate. For example, within twelve months of the 9/11 attacks on the World Trade Center, the Museum of the City of New York helped identify artifacts from Ground Zero that would be preserved for future generations, created an online memorial to the victims, set up a visual archive of ten thousand images documenting the recovery of Ground Zero, and organized a traveling exhibition based on the images. The museum also organized an exhibition on Arab American New Yorkers. Moscow City Museum has organized an exhibition on terrorist attacks on Moscow and one on new buildings in the city, without captions, leaving visitors to draw their own conclusions on the city's urban development. In Copenhagen, developers are required by the city council to consult the city museum, which is a repository of knowledge about city history, before undertaking major works. Museums in Helsinki, Stockholm, and Amsterdam are involved in similar engagements with contemporary life. They are very far from being alone.

It would be wrong to refer to a revolution among city museums (museum people are not, on the whole, revolutionaries), but this relatively new museum of the city that looks beyond the safety of the city's past to the uncertainties of the present and even to the uncharted waters of the future has become increasingly common. It is a museum about the city in all its aspects, not a museum that happens to be in the city. Its subject is the city: This is its only artifact. This artifact is, however, alive, all around the museum, and relentlessly changing. You cannot put it in a glass case.

In 1993 a conference of city museums was held at the Museum of London. It was very probably the first international symposium on museums about cities, and a loose grouping of museums about cities took shape— the International Association of City Museums. Subsequent meetings were held in Barcelona in 1995, in Luxembourg in 2000, and in Amsterdam in 2005. In 1995 an issue of UNESCO's *Museum International* was devoted largely to city museums.[11] It contained two seminal articles: "Discovering the City" by Nichola Johnson, then director of Museology at the University of East Anglia in England, and "Museums about Cities" by Max Hebditch, then director of the Museum of London. If there was indeed a new city museums movement, these two articles could be said to encapsulate its rationale. Later, the 2005 Amsterdam conference gathered its proceedings under the title of *City Museums as Centers of Civic Dialogue?*[12]

In Moscow in 2005, the inaugural meeting took place of CAMOC, the new international committee referred to earlier. Its impetus came from a need felt by a number of museum people for a more formal arrangement than had been the case with the informal International Association of City Museums. Galina Vedernikova, director of the Moscow City Museum, became chairperson of this new committee. The committee broke fresh ground in that it was to be a forum not only for museum professionals, but also for architects, urban planners, historians, sociologists, geographers—indeed, for anyone with an interest and involvement in the city.

All this reflects the regained importance of cities in national and world affairs, and the fact that half of the world's population now lives in cities, towns, and suburbs. It also reflects shifting attitudes to the city around the museum and ways of representing and interpreting it inside the museum's walls: The city is worthy of examination, and that means a bit more than presenting the city's history in a case or on an exhibition board. Then there is perhaps a greater recognition than before that city museums are dealing not just with city treasures, but with the lives of people and their interaction with each other and with their urban environment.

A city's history should be easier to deal with than its present, in that we have the advantage of distance: We can look back and assess our city's history objectively. Or can we? Frankly, it is impossible to be totally dispassionate and objective, and city history can be political dynamite in some places. Distance can have the habit of lending enchantment to the eye and providing a view of past centuries that is unjustified by the facts as we know

FIGURE 1.3
Seoul Museum of History, a museum for a city of about ten million people, far more if you include all its suburbs, and with a history stretching back for centuries. © Seoul Museum of History.

them. Nostalgia can be irresistible, especially if it applies to the recent past. In Britain, as the great industries of coal, steel, and tinplate went into terminal decline, so a concept like heritage arose to become, bizarrely, an industry in itself employing large numbers of people, presenting an account of past events that frequently bore a distorted relationship to reality; the poverty and hardships of the past were often only alluded to and then only in a somewhat sanitized form. It is a reflection, at least in Britain, of an obsession, as the contemporary historian Tony Judt has put it, with the way things weren't.[13] In Germany, a country with a traumatic past by any standard, Edgar Rietz's 1984 TV series *Heimat: Eine deutsche Chronik* attracted an average of nine million viewers, and the prevalent *Ostalgie* (almost an affection for the former German Democratic Republic) taps into the human capacity, to quote Tony Judt again, "for selective nostalgia for whatever might be retrieved from the detritus of lost pasts."[14] The way we were is a powerful drug, and heritage becomes an industry, simply because there is a market for it. Again, the facts may be hard to find or nonexistent, and we can only guess about the real nature of particular past lives and past conditions. As the Welsh politician Aneurin Bevan put it once, "You tell me your truth, and I'll tell you mine."

The present is a different challenge in that it is happening now and changing all the time; it is out there in the streets of the city, not inside the museum walls. There are none of the advantages of hindsight—the past at least has happened. What artifacts should we collect that properly reflect the city today? What is significant for future generations?

On the other hand, we cannot easily separate the past from the present and the future: one flows into the other. There are sometimes violent, abrupt, traumatic transitions, but there are no completely separate chapters. After all, the past was once the present, and we are creating our future every day. What may seem quaint to us now was not so at the time. Everything under the sun has been modern in its day, and we may well appear quaint to future generations. And the city's past, like its present, is all around us; we see it every day in the city's fabric. It has shaped our present as our present will shape our future. The past is inside us, too; we have our own histories. After all, where would we be without recollection of past events? As Chateaubriand wrote so lyrically:

> And yet, what would we be without memory? We would not be capable of ordering even the simplest thoughts, the most sensitive heart would lose the ability to show affection, our existence would be a mere never-ending chain of meaningless moments, and there would not be the faintest trace of a past.[15]

But can the museum do more than reflect and interpret the past and present? What about the development of the city—its future? Is that beyond the remit of the museum? Joseph Rykwert points out in his book on the city, *The Seduction of Place*, that we have only ourselves to blame if things get worse rather than better. How can we make things better, make our city worth living in, make it one that people don't want to leave? Rykwert suggests that "constant community participation and involvement are needed to shape our cities and to make them communicative, and this notion seems tragically to have been forgotten by the various bodies that govern us."[16]

What part could a museum play in all this? Duncan Grewcock, writing in an issue of *Museum International* devoted to city museums and based on CAMOC's first conference in Boston in 2006, put it this way:

> If museums of cities did not already exist, they might now need to be invented to help understand and negotiate urban change. The unique position that museums of cities could occupy within urban planning is represented by the qualitative difference of museum space as opposed to other kinds of public space or elements of the contemporary mediascape. That is, as an open-ended, trusted democratic space, that can be physically experienced as a quarter of the city, but also used as a site for debate, discussion and experimentation on urban issues within the context of a city's past, present and future. This would see museums of cities as a key element in the narrative of the city and as part of its ongoing story of becoming: the museum as a networked, distributed conversation rather than an inward-looking institution.[17]

A museum about a city is, or should be, a repository of knowledge about the city's past. It can therefore be a unique resource for the better understanding of the city's present. Not only that, it can provide an informed platform for planning the city's future. In so doing, it can also be a forum for debate and discussion to enable city people to contribute actively to their city's development. Knowing and understanding the city is the first step to changing it for the better—and helping to know and understand is what museums are good at. Nichola Johnson, writing in *Museum International* in 1995, put it well:

> The best city museums act as a starting-point for the discovery of the city, which can lead people to look with fresh, more informed and more tolerant eyes at the richness of the present urban environment and to imagine beyond it to past and possible future histories.[18]

That is what this book is about. The background is provided by Georges Prévélakis's chapter on city museums and the geopolitics of globalization: the renaissance of the city set against the relative decline of the nation-state and the rise of the process of international integration we refer to as globalization. Globalization may not be an altogether new phenomenon, but it has been given massive impetus by the Internet and the worldwide communications network. What is happening to our sense of place in this increasingly homogenized world? In his book *The New Town Square*, Robert Archibald asserts:

> The most profound dilemma of this new century, inherited from the last, is a deepening crisis of place and the accompanying ennui of placelessness. Lack of attachment to place disembodies memory, sunders relationships, promotes prodigal resource consumption; it threatens democracy itself, which so much depends upon those "mystic chords of memory" and habits that bind us to one another in a shared pursuit of the common good. . . . When we lose those places, we lose an essential part of ourselves and our stories.[19]

FIGURE 1.4
Model of the proposed city museum of Chengdu, capital of Sichuan Province,
South West China. Sutherland Hussey Architects in collaboration with Pansolution
International Design. © Sutherland Hussey Architects.

Chapters on museums of the cities of Stuttgart, Taipei, Sydney, and
Kazan illustrate how new and existing museums deal with this sense of
place and identity. Each museum has a set of priorities, policies, problems,
and opportunities shaped by its relationship to city government, to national and local politics, and to the particular features of the city. In contrast, Max Hebditch looks at museums in small towns, so often forgotten
when we talk about our new urban world—places like Robert Archibald's
hometown of Ishpeming in Michigan, USA. In spite of our infatuation
with megacities, most urban living takes place in relatively small cities and
towns. What can a museum do to reinforce the distinctive character of
these places, when they are up against the dominating city a few kilometers
down the motorway? Jack Lohman uses the examples of Dublin and London to deal with the question so many of us have asked: Why is it that city
museums often seem as if the city had departed? London's major airport,

he points out, has more employees than a large English city; Dublin, a small capital city, has more Poles per capita than the world city of London. How can we represent this city reality we see around us?

Eric Sandweiss traces the illuminating history of historical societies and city museums in the United States, glances at Vienna (a city so like a museum it ought perhaps to be in one), and takes note of the contemporary city museum, equipped as it so frequently is with tools designed for other jobs and other times, not those designed for the city of change, unpredictability, and social fluidity. Chet Orloff proposes that city museums have an obligation to play a significant part in urban and regional planning, and with their own specific knowledge and expertise they can, through partnerships and an international network, make profound contributions to their own community and others. Geoffrey Edwards and Marie Louise Bourbeau look at city museums in a society characterized by what they term peripheralization, a world with fewer well-defined boundaries, and a

FIGURE 1.5
The vast expanse of Mexico City, a challenge for any museum of a city to encapsulate. The photo is taken from the Venice Biennale international architecture exhibition of 2006: Cities, Architecture, and Society. Curated by Richard Burdett, Centennial Professor in Architecture and Urbanism at the London School of Economics, it dealt with the problems and possibilities of sixteen cities across the world through photography, film, and mixed media. It was an object lesson for museums in presenting cities in all their aspects and bringing a great array of statistics to life in a vivid and intelligent way. © Armin Linke.

less homogeneous cultural environment where the individual has many identities, not just one. Then there is the virtual world, one in which museums must operate as much as they do in the physical world. This is one theme taken up by Marlen Mouliou in her chapter on museums in the Internet age. Her chapter also provides us with a survey of city museum operations today.

Then there is the environment. What intelligent statement can a museum about a city make about global warming and environmentally sustainable development in the city? What can a museum contribute to, say, Curitiba in Brazil, frequently described as the most environmentally innovative city in the world? Curitiba at least has a history going back to the seventeenth century. But what about one of the new ecocities like Dongtan, under construction on the world's largest alluvial island in the Yangtze River delta near Shanghai? A city of eighty-six square kilometers is envisaged with a population of half a million by 2040. The first section is scheduled for completion in 2010, with a population of twenty-five thousand. In dramatic contrast to Shanghai there will be zero pollution, few if any cars, and energy will be renewable—a green utopia in other words.[20] It will have no history—not yet, anyway—but it will have a future. What can a museum make of it? A lot, one day. In essence, Dongtan is another Saint Petersburg. That, too, was created out of nothing—and look at it today. Its history is sensational. But what can a museum do now about a city like Dongtan? That could be the subject of another book.

NOTES

1. John Reader, *Cities* (London: Heinemann, 2004), 1.

2. J. John Palen, *The Urban World* (New York: McGraw-Hill, 1975), 3.

3. Joel Kotkin, *The City: A Global History* (London: Weidenfield & Nicholson, 2005), 160.

4. *State of the World's Cities 2006/7* (Nairobi: United Nations Human Settlements Program UN-HABITAT, 2006). Downloaded copy, not numbered. See also United Nations Department of Economic and Social Affairs, Population Division, www.un.org/esa/population/unpop.htm.

5. *Financial Times*, 27 July 2004; David Drakakis-Smith, *Third World Cities*, 2nd ed. (London: Routledge, 2000), quoted in Mike Davis, *Planet of Slums* (London: Verso, 2006), 2.

6. Ricky Burdett and Deyan Sudjic, eds., *The Endless City: The Urban Age Project by the London School of Economics and the Deutsche Bank's Alfred Herrhausen Society* (London: Phaidon, 2007), 19.

7. *Pocket World in Figures, 2008 Edition* (London: *The Economist*, 2007), 22. *State of the World's Cities 2006/7*. See also the comprehensive data on cities by the United Nations Department of Economic and Social Affairs, Population Division.

8. *World in Figures, 2008*, 23.

9. *State of the World's Cities, 2001* (Nairobi: United Nations Human Settlements Program UN-HABITAT, 2001). Quoted in a separate summary of the report, downloaded copy. Not numbered.

10. New Economics Foundation, *Clone Town Britain* (London: New Economics Foundation, 2005), 2. This report makes a distinction between a hometown and what the authors describe as a clone town:

> A *home* town is a place that retains its individual character and is instantly recognizable and distinctive to the people who live there, as well as those who visit. A *clone town* is a place that has had the individuality of its high street shops replaced by a monochrome strip of global and national chains that means its retail heart could easily be mistaken for dozens of other bland town centers across the country.

11. Nichola Johnson, "Discovering the City," *Museum International*, no. 187, vol. 47, no. 3 (July–September 1995): 4–6. Max Hebditch, "Museums about Cities," *Museum International* , no. 187, vol. 47, no. 3 (July–September 1995): 7–11.

12. Renée Kistemaker, ed., *City Museums as Centers of Civic Dialogue? Proceedings of the Fourth Conference of the International Association of City Museums, 3–5 November 2005* (Amsterdam: Amsterdam Historical Museum, 2006).

13. Tony Judt, *Post-War, a History of Europe since 1945* (London: Pimlico Random House, 2007), 768–774.

14. Judt, *Post-War*, 769.

15. From *Mémoires d'Outre-Tombe* by Chateaubriand, quoted in W. G. Sebald, *The Rings of Saturn* (London: Vintage, 2002), 255.

16. Joseph Rykwert, *The Seduction of Place: The History and Future of the City* (Oxford: Oxford University Press, 2000), 246.

17. Duncan Grewcock, "Museums of Cities and Urban Futures: New Approaches to Urban Planning and the Opportunities for Museums of Cities," *Museum International*, no. 231, vol. 58, no. 3 (September 2006): 40.

18. Johnson, "Discovering the City," 6.

19. Robert R. Archibald, *The New Town Square: Museums and Communities in Transition* (Walnut Creek, CA: AltaMira Press, 2004), 1.

20. Fred Pearce, "Master Plan," *New Scientist*, June 2006, 43–45.

2

City Museums and the Geopolitics of Globalization

Georges Prévélakis

Political geography is traditionally interested in the ways that geographical space is partitioned. Territories and borders constitute a major part of its literature. Since the Second World War, its interests have been enlarged to cover not only the territorial organization of the world but also geographical networks: the systems of interconnection of small but important territories like cities or islands.

The influence of the *circulation* factor comes first to our attention when we try to analyze the dynamics of geographical space. Circulation is at the basis of the exchange of goods; of migrations; of the diffusion of ideas, techniques, or values. It is a factor of change, of innovation, of freedom, of wealth. It can, however, also be a factor of destabilization and even of destruction. The barbarian invasions in Europe in the Middle Ages or the disappearance of Indian textile manufacture under the competition of imports from England during the nineteenth century are also expressions of the circulation factor. Today, the brutal introduction of the Western cultural model is destabilizing traditionalist Mediterranean societies, the result of which is not only local struggles for freedom but also global terrorism.

Facing the destructive influences of circulation, a balancing power must therefore exist, otherwise it would be difficult to explain the survival and continuity of human communities and their capacity to combine innovation with accumulation. Jean Gottmann named this factor iconography.[1] He described it as society's self-defense mechanism against destabilization by circulation—a "glue" linking the members of a community with each other and with a parcel of geographical space. Iconographies are at the foundation of territoriality, of the partitioning of geographical space, of the distinction between "us" and "them." They are made up of cultural elements, the most obvious of which are language, religion, and history. Behind those aggregate forms are hidden smells and sounds, landscapes and architectures, myths and rituals. All those icons are constantly being reinterpreted and reorganized in order to provide the necessary adaptation of iconographies to changing geopolitical conditions. The icons themselves, which evolve very slowly or not at all, provide societies with the element of continuity; their reshuffling introduces the element of change.

Various institutions function as iconographic laboratories or as instruments for the diffusion of iconographies. In premodern societies, religious institutions were paramount. During the last two centuries, academic institutions have played the first role, the army and the school the second. A network of other institutions, like the press and later the media, also contributed to the overall effort.

Museums have also been a major player in the production and diffusion of iconography. By the selection of the objects they present, they express a certain vision of the world. Thus, for example, ethnographic museums, by displaying objects selected according to geographic criteria, construct mental political maps—conservative if they coincide with the existing order, revisionist if they do not.

Museums therefore have a considerable responsibility, and their ethical problems are not very different from those of historiography. How can objectivity and scientific deontology be combined with the inevitable political role? There can be no universal answer to this question. However, the more such issues are discussed, the more the snares of conservativism, manipulation, and instrumentalization can be avoided.

What is the position of museums about cities in this debate? In comparison to historical, ethnographic, art, or even natural science or technology museums, it seems that they play a secondary role. History, ethnography, and art are directly related to national myths; natural science and technology have much to do with national pride ("our" nature or "our" technology). Per se, museums about cities do not seem related to national iconography. The cities they represent appear as a passive background to the actions of other actors, most often kings or national elites, and quite often a visit to a museum about a city leaves a sense of heterogeneity, of collections without internal cohesion.

This remark has to be tempered in the face of the great diversity of museums. However, independently of the greater or lesser talent of museum managers, museums about cities do have a structural handicap in comparison with other, more popular museums. To understand the causes of this handicap, the geopolitics of cities needs to be analyzed.

THE WORLD OF CITIES, FROM CENTRALITY TO MARGINALIZATION

Cities have long been the structural components of space partitioning. The Greek world was made up of city-states. Connected by sea routes, Greek cities constituted geographical networks that created larger political entities, more or less stable, in the form of federations of city-states. The Roman Empire extended the Greek maritime networks inland, and centralized and stabilized them. It did not challenge the territorial primacy of the city. This iconographic situation still survives: The building block of Orthodox Christianity is always the metropolis.

The process that started with the collapse of the western part of the Roman Empire led, after more than a thousand years, to a new geopolitical order in which the city-state was replaced by the territorial nation-state. In the nineteenth century, this historical process had achieved full maturity. The city in the West was definitively subjugated to the state. From territory, it became space—urban space. Those new urban spaces were determined by external logics: nationalism, the Industrial Revolution, colonialism.

The process of transition of cities from geopolitical centrality to marginality was not linear. For centuries the city spirit struggled in Europe against the ethos of the territorial state. The heritage of cities is thus the essence of Europe. If states express the tendency toward European fragmentation, cities symbolize the aspiration of European unity. The Italian Renaissance cities or the cities of the Hansa Teutonicorum are as much the predecessors of the European Union as the monarchies of England or France. Outside Europe, Singapore and Hong Kong developed a territorial status that reminds us of the Hanseatic League. They constitute the exceptions that confirm the rule.

Modernity, the new geopolitical and geoeconomic organization, marginalized the city politically and spiritually, even if it created the conditions for an unprecedented and continuous urbanization. The character of the cities changed substantially. Inside them, socioeconomic cleavages (bourgeoisie/proletariat) replaced the old ethno-economic divisions.

As Western modernity conquered new spaces, many cities became national capitals, focal points of nationalism. Other cities, often important crossroads of diasporas, were turned into spaces of industrial production or, more often, into marginalized peripheries of the national capital. In many cases, those changes took violent and tragic forms. Salonika, Izmir, and Alexandria are among the eastern Mediterranean cities that lost the most active part of their population during the twentieth century and are left today with deep traumas and strong feelings of guilt. Similar cases can be found in central and eastern Europe.

Under such circumstances, what could museums express during the nineteenth and the twentieth centuries? City history in the West was usually the story of the defeat of the city authorities by monarchies, states, or nations. In more traumatic situations, city museums were obliged to function in a context of self-censorship and generalized amnesia. In the postcolonial context, the city often represented the focal point of the colonial past, also to be forgotten.

GLOBALIZATION AND THE CITY

Thus, during the past two centuries, in spite of the tremendous importance of events that happened inside urban spaces, the city had ceased to be a political actor. It rarely could develop a proper iconography.

However, during the second half of the twentieth century, at the same time as the last remaining "traditional" cities were succumbing to the pressure of the territorial nation-state, the world started changing rapidly. Globalization started as an economic trend, which also gradually became cultural and political. The end of the Cold War confirmed and consolidated the unification of geographical space. Globalization is nothing else than the explosive growth of circulation on the scale of the globe. Its main target is the fragmentation of space into territorial states.

Thus, soon after its triumph, the territorial nation-state is being challenged at its very foundations. The U.S. declarations during the Yugoslav wars that the respect of state sovereignty does not have priority over the duty of humanitarian intervention gave the measure of the changes that had taken place, not only in the fields of technology and economic relations, but also in the minds of people.

We live in a period of change that is fascinating but also very dangerous. The extreme destabilization produced by successive waves of globalization creates the need to develop new modes of stability, adapted to new conditions. As national iconographies are weakening, new forms of iconographies are being tried out. The change in scale produced by space-shrinking technologies (air transport, fast trains, telecommunications) leads to a search for iconographies of enlarged spaces—the European project corresponds to this trend. At the same time, at the opposite end of the scale, regional and city iconographies are also rapidly reappearing.

The return of city iconographies has very solid foundations in the actual restructuring of geographical space. Recent technological innovations have created the possibility of overcoming distance and therefore bypassing the principle of spatial contiguity. Important cities—and especially global cities—are interconnected and function as geographical networks. Linkages with cities outside the national territory can and do become more important than connections with cities belonging to the same state, or even with the cities' traditional rural hinterland.

Many geographers have compared this evolving situation to *archipelaga*. Cities are seen as islands emerging out of seas of rurality, connected among themselves in the same way that sea routes link islands. This analogy leads to other historical parallels. The city archipelago of globalization is animated by diaspora networks, as happened in the traditional networks of the Mediterranean world's *emporia*. Thus cities again become crossroads of diasporas. After a long period of ethnic simplification, migrations and the new economic opportunities related to globalization are reconstituting cultural diversity inside cities. Through an irony of history, at the same time as old mixed-population cities—like Sarajevo recently—were subjected to ethnic cleansing, paradigmatic national capitals like Paris or London became collections of the ethnic groups of the world.

In their efforts to attract capital, talent, and international attention, cities are in competition on the global stage. They rely to a large extent on their image. Culture becomes an essential asset. The regeneration of old neighborhoods is at least as important as the construction of the new architectural icons of globalization. The fierce international competition to host the Olympic Games is an illustration of new forms of competition in which the city is taking the initiative.

Cities are today in the forefront of new opportunities and dangers. Their growing global role creates responsibilities at a moment when the world is under stress through the generalization of circulation, while national and international institutions appear more and more irrelevant and inefficient. In order to promote new forms of cooperation between cultures, cities need to invent and to propose new cultural and political models. They are in an excellent position to become laboratories of the "dialogue of civilizations," in order to counterbalance the effects of the "conflict of civilizations" raging in the surrounding sea of the global archipelago. Regional integration projects like that of the European Union also rely strongly on city and city-networks initiatives. European cities linked together may promote European unity more efficiently than efforts to create new European institutions.

Global changes are influencing urban space, creating new tensions and contradictions very different from those of the industrial city of the past. The growth of a dynamic cosmopolitan urban class—living much more in the archipelagic global network than inside the national territory and often participating in diasporic identities—is remodeling urban space. Old industrial neighborhoods, often situated in privileged physical settings—in contact with rivers or the sea—are becoming grounds of competition among residual working classes, marginalized groups, and the new rising cosmopolitan class. Even if in Western societies social protection offers a security net to the most unfortunate, the cultural and educational divide is introducing new forms of exclusion, of resentment, of social stress. The poor neighborhoods or suburbs, largely occupied by immigrants, are not parts of the archipelago; their inhabitants consider themselves belonging rather to the darkness of deep seas. Urban riots or terrorist networks illustrate the dangers related to a rapidly changing urban environment. It took almost a century for Western societies to adapt to the tensions related to the emergence of the industrial city. In the context of deindustrialization and globalization, the solutions found and implemented in the framework of national policies some decades ago are now obsolete.

CITY MUSEUMS AND CITY ICONOGRAPHY

Cities need to respond to the new challenges by reestablishing their status as actors. There are institutions that represent and respond to this need, like municipalities or metropolitan administrative structures. Residues of a past city autonomy that has been gradually marginalized by the strengthening of the state and by urban growth or the creations of the state through top-down processes of decentralization, these institutions are gradually acquiring more initiative and strength. Paris exemplifies the new trends. A new era in the relationship between city and state began with the election of Jacques Chirac as mayor of Paris in 1977. Within a few years, he had transformed the municipality into a center of countervailing power against socialist governments. Indeed, Chirac initiated a tradition of using the office of mayor of the capital city as a stepping-stone to national government leadership. Other city leaders took note. Miltiadis Evert, the mayor of Athens in the late 1980s, tried to copy Chirac and move from city to national leadership; he managed to become the leader of his party in 1993, but lost the elections twice and had to resign from the party leadership in 1997. Recep Tayyip Erdogan, the current prime minister of Turkey, was previously mayor of Istanbul. The current mayor of Paris, Bertrand Delanoë, is the most probable challenger to Nicolas Sarkozy in the next French presidential election in 2012.

In the new partitioning of the world that is taking shape in front of our eyes, the city scale is becoming essential again. Its reinforcement is an important task because it can contribute to stabilizing a world threatened by chaos. Cities can constitute the building blocks for regional complexes inspired more by the model of the Roman Empire than by that of the territorial nation-state.

The return of cities on the political scene will not happen, however, by itself. In parallel with the economic, political, and administrative processes, it is necessary to elaborate and to promote the iconographies that will unify the actors concerned with city destinies and create new forms of solidarity based on the city.

The process of iconographic production, reproduction, and diffusion cannot be dictated from above. To succeed it has to rely on already existing social capital and benefit from a favorable geopolitical context. The role of personalities—intellectual, artistic, or political—cannot be underestimated either. It is the mix of all these components that determines the success of an iconographic project.

Today cities are entering the arena of iconographic competition. For this reason, museums about cities from being marginal are becoming central. They can and will become the forums of iconographic exploration, the crucibles of iconographic construction, and the focal points of iconographic diffusion. If they do not grasp the opportunity, other institutions or organizations will emerge to do it in their place.

Their task will be to bring together the various elements of city history that the previous period dispersed, in order to demonstrate their essential unity, based on the spirit of place. City museums must reconstruct the memories of city autonomy or independence. They must stress the importance of those periods of city history when the city did constitute a political entity, the story of its struggles against other political actors—kings, empires, nations.

At the same time, museums of cities need to illustrate and defend the openness of the city, its inclusion in larger networks of cities, the linkages that connect it to the world. It is necessary to shift the geographical imagination from the center-periphery model—stressing the relationship between the city and its hinterland—toward the network model, showing how cities are vital nodes of circulation and form larger, nonterritorial geographical entities. The changes in the architecture of those networks during different periods—from empires to nation-states, for example—is useful as an indication of how certain relationships could, and perhaps should, be reestablished.

This new mental mapping will also have important consequences in the perception of city space and society. As part of transterritorial geographic networks, cities were hubs of transnational economic and social networks—diaspora crossroads. Cultural heterogeneity is the historical norm for the city, homogeneity being the exception. By reminding ourselves of this fact, today's problems of xenophobia and racism can be discussed in the light of a more positive perspective. At the same time, cities can create networks of friendship and solidarity with nostalgic outside communities that have historical roots in the city in question.

These historical, cultural, and geopolitical themes and issues constitute a field of iconographic innovation of extraordinary wealth. By selecting the most relevant icons from this field and by combining them into new narratives, city museums can participate in the invention of new forms of space partitioning. They can play an important role in the search for a new balance between freedom and stability, between opportunity and security, between circulation and iconography. Those new challenges must lead to the development of a new vision for museums about cities—and dialogue, comparing experiences, and cooperation between museums are essential.

The materiality of city space, the solidarities of cohabitation, constitute an essential remedy for the vertigo of the open seas of globalization. In the archipelago of cities, the Collections and Activities of Museums of Cities (CAMOC), the new international committee established by the Paris-based International Council of Museums, has to become a forum whose role should be not only to encourage the development of city iconographies, but also to promote the emergence of an iconography of city networks. Contrary to the ideology of globalization, this archipelagic iconography will not sacrifice rootedness, the sense of place, and the sense of belonging to openness.

NOTE

1. For a short presentation of Gottmann's ideas and their geopolitical implications, see Georges Prévélakis, "The Relevance of Jean Gottmann in Today's World," *Ekistics* 422 (September–October 2003): 295–304. For the first presentation of the concept of iconography in English, see Jean Gottmann, "Geography and International Relations," *World Politics* 2, no. 2 (January 1951): 153–173, 163, followed by a more detailed analysis in Jean Gottmann, "The Political Partitioning of Our World: An Attempt at Analysis," *World Politics* 4, no. 4 (July 1952): 512–519, 516.

BIBLIOGRAPHY

Castells, Manuel. "European Cities, the Informational Society and the Global Economy." In *Understanding Amsterdam: Essays on Economic Vitality, City Life and Urban Form*, edited by Léon Deben, Willem Heinemeijer, and Dick van der Vaar, 7–23. Amsterdam: Hen Spinhuis, 1993.

Claval, Paul. "The Cultural Dimension in Restructuring Metropolises: The Amsterdam Example." In *Understanding Amsterdam: Essays on Economic Vitality, City Life, and Urban Form*, edited by Léon Deben, Willem Heinemeijer, and Dick van der Vaar, 111–139. Amsterdam: Hen Spinhuis, 1993.

Cosaert, Patrice. "East Asia: An Example of Regional Integration via Networks and Flows." In *Cities and Networks in Europe: A Critical Approach of Polycentrism*, edited by Nadine Catan, 199–207. Esher, Surrey, UK: John Libbey, Eurotext, 2007.

Davie, Michael F. "National Versus Regional and International Networking in the Arab World." In *Cities and Networks in Europe: A Critical Approach of Polycentrism*, edited by Nadine Catan, 189–198. Esher, Surrey, UK: John Libbey, Eurotext, 2007.

Gottmann, Jean. "Geography and International Relations" *World Politics* 2, no. 2 (January 1951): 153–173.

———. *Megalopolis: The Urbanized Northeastern Seaboard of the United States.* New York: The Twentieth Century Fund, 1961.

———. "The Political Partitioning of Our World: An Attempt at Analysis." *World Politics* 4, no. 4 (July 1952): 512–519.

———. *The Significance of Territory.* Charlottesville: University Press of Virginia, 1973.

Parker, Geoffrey. "Vers une nouvelle hanse: metropoles et nations dans la géographie politique de l'Europe." In *Métropolisation et politique*, edited by Paul Claval and André-Louis Sanguin, 27–36. Paris: L'Harmattan, 1997.

Prévélakis, Georges. "Culture, Politics, and the Urban Crisis: The Case of Modern Athens." *Modern Greek Studies Yearbook* 5 (1989): 1–32.

———. "Les grandes métropoles comme carrefours des diasporas." *Cybergeo*, August 11, 1997. www.cybergeo.eu/index1169.html.

———. "Istanbul, Skopje et Salonique: villes-frontières ou cités-carrefours?" In *L'Europe et ses villes frontières*, edited by Joël Kotek, 77–96. Brussels: Complexe, 1996.

———. "The Relevance of Jean Gottmann in Today's World." *Ekistics* 422 (September–October 2003): 295–304.

Sassen, Saskia. *The Global City: New York, London, Tokyo.* Princeton, NJ: Princeton University Press, 2001.

3

Museums of Cities and the Future of Cities

CHET ORLOFF

The future . . . lies in collaboration across borders, cultures, [city museums], and disciplines.[1]

The nineteenth century was, broadly speaking, the century of the history and the natural history museum, an era of exploration and a fitting time for the growth and popularity of "cabinets of curiosities." The twentieth century was very much the century of the art museum, a time of building deep collections and great buildings, with far-ranging advances in the visual arts. The twenty-first century—when cities will be, even more, the places where people live and where so much will happen—ought to be the moment of the city museum. The future? It is our time.

With vast knowledge at our command, with rich experience in education and public programming, with our own and fellow museums' collective resources readily accessible, city museums—especially working collaboratively across borders and over the Web—are positioned to help resolve, in some cases even pose, issues of historic import to our communities.

All this has been said before, in countless conferences and conversations. Why do we hear it repeated? Because, with very few exceptions, city museums have yet to take concerted, collaborative, and coordinated action. Now, with the establishment of an international body of city museums, we have the opportunity to cocreate exhibits and educational programs that will serve our own and each others' cities in ways unimaginable only five years ago.[2]

With the creation of the International Council of Museums' Committee for the Collections and Activities of Museums of Cities (CAMOC), city museums are poised to make even more significant contributions to their own and the world's cities. Having created, through CAMOC, a structure and coalition—a community of organizations versed in and richly endowed with materials and knowledge that inform urban affairs—city museums must enlarge their collective scope to encompass not just the stewardship of urban history, but the planning and shaping of the venues they share, the world's cities.

Planning presumes knowledge of a place as well as a clear sense of its identity—in other words, an ability to confidently offer convincing answers to such questions as the following: Who are its people? What are their aspirations? Why and how might the community differ from others? Where are its significant historic and contemporary sites? When have its notable events occurred? Knowing these facts (and fables) is not, of course, the assignment of planners only, nor of the elected and appointed officials they serve. Such knowledge is the province of museums of cities, and they should be active—in some cases, even aggressive—in sharing it with every agency, organization, and individual involved in community planning.

The twenty-first century is emerging as, among other things, an urban era, with more than half the world's people living in cities. Globalization is accompanied by urbanization, as regional, national, and international economies grow technologically. This is hardly new; industrialization in the nineteenth century began the process of urbanization in earnest. As places to study and learn from, cities present our museums with unparalleled opportunities for interpretation. Equally, as places in great need of the best planning, cities offer our museums great obligations to best inform such planning and even to initiate projects that challenge our cities.

As great artistic and historical entities of the nineteenth century, and as elemental political, social, and economic entities of the twentieth century, cities have much to tell us about the nature of the twenty-first century and about the ever more difficult times we are now entering. And as vital and engaged members of our communities, our job as urban curators is not merely to collect and share historical knowledge, but to help change and shape the lives of our cities and their citizens—a transformative function that the psychiatrists of Vienna, one of Europe's significant cities, would certainly have appreciated.[3] Indeed, those of us working for the institutions curating our cities are very much like the great psychiatrists of that city—our work is to help cities understand themselves and, acting on that understanding, lead better and healthier lives.

THE CHALLENGE

As a professional museum director and amateur planner, I have spent as much of my career looking into my city's future as into its past.[4] When I conceived the Museum of the City in 2001—on September 10, to be exact—the idea was to establish a museum that would look at my home (Portland, Oregon) and *other* cities from the perspective of urban history and urban planning. In other words, we would explore the development, design, and future of *the* city, not just the city of Portland. Hence, my interest in other cities and what they could tell mine, and each other, about the past, present, and, especially, the future of cities worldwide. I believe that many colleagues and our patrons share this interest, so I will proceed.

A pivotal question for me and my founding colleagues (all planners with deep roots in historic preservation) was, and remains: What is the responsibility of the Museum of the City in supporting urban planning in our own and other cities? We began with the knowledge, from professional experience, that urban planning plays three essential functions in a community: (1) understanding a city's past development, (2) managing its current design, and (3) planning its future. Knowing this, I pose the following question to colleagues in city museums elsewhere: What is the responsibility of city museums, more generally, in supporting these functions in their own and others' cities?

My answer to this larger question, and the substance of this chapter, is that (1) city museums have an obligation—more than merely an opportunity—to play significant and meaningful roles in urban and regional planning; and (2) city museums, working collaboratively within dynamic partnerships and an international network, can apply the capabilities and knowledge they hold within their staffs and collections to make profound contributions to their own and others' communities.

I am not suggesting here that city museums become planning agencies themselves. What I am suggesting is that through combining resources, our museums serve our cities as integral sources of historical knowledge about planning and as proactive providers of insight for current planning. To fulfill this role, city museums must be conveners, bringing together members of their community as well as colleagues from sister city museums around the discussion *not only* about their city's past and present, but about their city's future as well. Even though much of our work pertains to the past, many museums worldwide have brought their community together around issues relating to its future. As such, many museums already serve as conveners, as "facilitators of the conversation," in Robert Archibald's words, about *who* the community's members are, *how* museums contribute to their community's life, and *what* matters to its citizens.[5] That conversation includes many diverse organizations and individuals.

SOME GIVENS

Why *should* city museums be conveners and active partners in the complex and often conflicting process of urban planning? The following reasons are derived from personal experience and conversations with colleagues within the museum and planning professions. I will be so bold as to consider them givens by those of us engaged in communities and charged with planning them.

The twenty-first is an urban century, and the solutions to the century's problems will be found in cities. As an increasingly fundamental political, social, and economic unit, the urban region will increasingly displace the nation-state as the basic unit of self-identification and culture. It will be increasingly in metropolitan regions that people will seek rootedness—a sense of place—and their own sense of community. To address the challenges of the century will require the involvement and contributions of all institutions with intellectual resources relating to urban issues. Leaders among such institutions are city museums. The relative importance of the role of museums about a city in helping citizens understand their place— a role most city museums already do well—will increase accordingly.

Planning the future is part of the DNA of cities. Just as surely as the lives of citizens in Etruscan farming towns were fundamentally altered by the planning of new Roman cities, so lives around the world will continue to be changed by urbanization and by good or bad urban planning. Just as collecting the past was and will certainly continue to be important for city museums, so museum programs about planning the future must become a significant and growing part of city museums' educational and programmatic agendas. If citizens aren't already demanding the attention of city museums to planning, then through our exhibits, public programs, and the participation of our staff in planning efforts, museums should be demanding the attention of citizens and their political leaders.

There are several kinds of organizations that contribute to urban planning—public planning agencies, architecture firms, consultants, museums, universities. They all provide perspective and technical insight. Of them all, which has the deepest well of information on how a region has gotten to where it is today? City museums, including our staffs, collections, and educational programs.

With all the challenges facing our metropolitan regions, we need better-informed regional planning. Cities can benefit from the knowledge that city museums have to offer about their community's history of planning and current aspirations. Even planners will admit that urban planning is too important to be left to planners alone; it is enriched by the experience and perspectives of the historians, curators, and educators affiliated with city museums.

Citizens in more and more countries will ultimately demand to be involved in urban planning. They will increasingly advocate that planning is not an exercise to be carried out by a professional elite, but an activity that affects people and their community and thus something in which they

FIGURE 3.1
Two different aspects of one city: Red Square, the iconic heart of Moscow, and a nearby building site, emblematic of a city changing almost by the day. One conclusion: A city is more than the sum of its historic components; too often city museums have concentrated on the iconic and historic at the expense of the mundane but vital aspects of city life. © Ian Jones.

must be involved. The best urban planning is done as a democratic process in which informed members of the public play a role. Museums are, by nature, democratic institutions—as much as if not more than other institutions—and our mission is to involve the public in our programs and support mechanisms. Technical as it is, planning can be seen as difficult to many citizens, if not threatening; they aren't generally comfortable with it. They are, generally, comfortable with museums. Museums can channel this comfort and confidence into the planning process by applying their public trust, educational strengths, storytelling and interpretive skills, and the public's familiarity with museums toward the often confusing and usually complex elements of planning.

One final thought about cities, city museums, planning, and the status quo: Through exhibits and other activities, city museums can enrich the public's experience about how *other* cities are designing and planning their futures, sharing perspectives from sister cities elsewhere. Citizens, not just their planners, need to see successes and failures from *elsewhere*, and city museums are appropriate venues, and often the only venues, for presenting such vivid information.

CONVENING THE CONVERSATION

In challenging city museums to be conveners for planning within our communities, it is appropriate to acknowledge how, in Archibald's words, we already "convene conversations" about the direction of our communities and, ultimately, about how an international network of museums might assist each other.

Traditionally, museums are collections-based. Increasingly, places, buildings, cities, and regions themselves are becoming the artifacts that city museums are preserving and interpreting, if not collecting, per se. Appropriately, city museums must look more and more beyond their own cataloged collections to the city itself, and to the individuals and buildings—and the ideas surrounding them—that animate the city. So, the challenge becomes, How can city museums take the urban environment itself and interpret it, literally, out on the street, within buildings, underground, and from the air?

Imagine the city itself within the exhibit case, and we're there, inside with it, interpreting it for the public. That is how I have explained to others the Museum of the City's motto: "The museum *is* the city; the city *is* the museum." What does this look like in reality? Richly interpretive guided tours, exhibits in public places, explanatory labels on buildings, and places described on cell phones and other handheld devices are just some of the ways the Museum of the City does it.

Museums, of course, have long exhibited beyond their own walls. Public places within the city offer appropriately relevant venues for unconventional approaches to interpreting urban planning. Recent locations for Museum of the City exhibits have included the Portland International Airport, the federal courthouse, houses of worship, corporate offices, the lobbies of major downtown buildings, and streetcar shelters.

While maintaining a healthy, objective, and disciplined perspective on their city, one aspect of the job of city museums is to make them *look* like their city. What does this mean? The more clearly city museums can reflect—through exhibits and other programs—the evolving personalities and shape of their city, the better they will mirror the changing face of their city while retaining and refreshing their relevance. To a degree, museums must be inseparable from their city. When you walk, ride, or fly into Portland or any city, so we envisioned, you have entered the Museum of the City.

Our outlook takes the old idea that the city and its buildings are our largest artifacts. It is an idea we should make universally understood. Then there is the practice of putting the entire city, in miniature, inside the museum. Numerous cities, in new planning museums and renovated city halls, have taken their cities inside by creating massive three-dimensional models by which to study, and promote, themselves. While not city museums as, perhaps, traditionally recognized, such endeavors certainly are opening new vistas for citizens to observe their urban environment.

How else can and do city museums convene the conversation around planning their community? The practice of urban planning draws on many disciplines and technical applications, including architecture and urban design, regional economics and economic development, real estate, trans-

portation planning, environmental science, mapping, history, and sociological analysis. These are all tools in the planning "tool kit." Museums can
add to this tool kit in important ways—they do communications and public outreach well, convey knowledge, present evocative images and stories,
offer perspective on how things have been done, and apply well-honed
skills at marshaling diverse concepts and making them understandable.

FIGURE 3.2
New Orleans, 2004. Old and new buildings provide opportunities for city museums to illuminate aspects of urban design and
the evolution of cities. © Chet Orloff.

If they aren't already, city museum professionals ought to be making themselves available to university urban planning programs as sources of knowledge about their cities and how to interpret them to the public. We are incredible resources, though we may not appreciate that. I offer my own experience as an example: While trained as a historian, I have spent much of my career serving the city of Portland as a planning commissioner and have recently put in hundreds of hours helping develop visions for the future of neighborhoods and for the city as a whole.

Considering what city museum staff know about their cities, participation in community planning activities through citizen advisory committees, public charrettes, and design exercises should be a core responsibility listed in the job description of every city museum director.

City museums and interpretive institutions focused on urban planning are refining their abilities at combining physical and digital information. Various forms of Internet postings about architecture and urban planning are additional means by which individuals and institutions share information and interpret the city to their citizens. By combining sound, documentary materials, and digital technology, city museums can create additional spaces—"virtual galleries"—in which to connect with and inform new audiences. I have been teaching courses recently in which the students have selected a location and then created cell phone and Web-based exhibits about its past and future, thereby combining history with planning. Not only have these been excellent learning opportunities for students, they have been provocative and refreshing sources of information for members of the public who visit these exhibits online.

Museums host conferences and symposia that bring planners, historians, designers, architects, and curators together. (In 2004, the Museum of the City organized a three-day citywide symposium on Portland to prepare citizens for a two-year visioning project undertaken by the new mayor.) City museums, I believe, should be enlisting the knowledge base represented among city museums internationally to enrich public planning meetings within our own and each other's communities.

Internet forums—blogs, wikis, message boards, discussion groups, listservs, bulletin boards—for holding discussions, and planning and running projects, have become customary within increasing numbers of industries, companies, and organizations. As tools for intermuseum project planning, however, city museum professionals have only begun to recognize their potential.

In listing these activities, I want to reiterate the suggestion that city museums even *more* actively share our assets and programs among ourselves. The experience of each other's cities is invaluable for planning purposes, and museums, among other attributes, have great experience in sharing. I, for one, look forward to future international meetings where members gather not only to discuss how to do our own work, but actually to plan and organize exhibits, conferences, tours, consultancies, and other endeavors for the benefit of our own and fellow members' cities.

Tools such as blogs, wikis, chat rooms, peer-to-peer networks, and personal broadcasting are putting unprecedented power in the hands of individual workers to communicate and collaborate more productively. This in turn is driving a new revolution in workplace collaboration of a qualitatively different nature. Having matured quickly in the last three years, these weapons of mass collaboration enable [city museum professionals] to engage and co-create with more people in more regions of the world.[6]

CONCLUSION

I began this discussion by posing the question: What is the responsibility of city museums in supporting urban planning in their own and others' cities? The answers bear repeating. First, city museums must increasingly leverage the qualities of trust, stewardship, knowledge, and experience that our community grants us to help bring community members to what I'll call the planning table. City museums belong there. It is around this table of interested, involved, *and* informed individuals and institutions that the direction affecting and effecting our regions' futures will be determined, and the input from city museums can be invaluable. Second, in order to best contribute to the planning of our community, individual city museums must act in concert, to collaborate in the cocreation of everything from exhibits and publications to conferences and other public programs. A body such as ICOM's CAMOC can help conduct such intermuseum collaboration.

City museums can and should play a critical role in urban planning. I mean "critical" here in two ways. First, we should be critical in the sense of engendering—of encouraging—serious dialogue that challenges our own city's prevailing assumptions about what and how to plan. This presumes a certain degree of knowledge—a knowledge that, I would argue, city museums possess in their staff, in their collections, and in the allied professionals they bring together for public programs. Second, I mean that we should be a critically—that is, an essentially—important player in catalyzing projects within our community. Again, this is a realm in which city museums have extensive experience, from organizing commemorations to instigating educational forums and teaching workshops.

There are a growing number of organizations—Washington, D.C.'s National Building Museum, the Shanghai and Beijing planning museums, the Pavillon de l'Arsenal in Paris, institutes of architecture—whose fundamental purpose is to interpret urban planning and architecture. Most of them focus their programs toward design and architectural themes. Most of these institutions are in major cities, though only a few major cities have them. City museums, however, are ubiquitous. We are in virtually *every* city and large town; many are in communities that may not even have planning agencies. Thus, we offer great potential for serving our communities as interpreters of, even leaders in, planning, especially if we use the collaborative and collective opportunities and intellectual power afforded by international organizations of city museums such as CAMOC.

Whatever the level of planning we involve ourselves in, we won't be charting a new course. Museums got an early start on urban planning. In the 1890s, the Musée Social was a French laboratory of urban thinking, marrying the museum's perspective to that of planning and social science. Soon after, the American John Cotton Dana staunchly advocated a role for museums in everything from planning neighborhoods to creating school curricula. The British planner Patrick Geddes's observatory was, in effect, a kind of museum experience of cities.

As Duncan Grewcock has explained, despite differing backgrounds and perspectives, museum professionals and planners are converging.[7] It will be up to the museum profession, however, to further extend this convergence, to engage planners in our concerted efforts to collaboratively curate our cities. Our audiences—the citizens of our communities—will be with us all the way. Our communities have put their trust in our ability to preserve their past and inform their perspectives on the present. All the more reason that they will put their faith—and their funds, I might add—in our ability to contribute to the shaping of their future.

NOTES

1. Don Tapscott and Anthony D. Williams, *Wikinomics: How Mass Collaboration Changes Everything* (New York: Portfolio, 2006), 61.

2. Tapscott and Williams, *Wikinomics*, 10.

3. Vienna served as the venue for the second annual CAMOC meeting. This chapter is based on a paper presented at that meeting.

4. Over the past thirty years, I have served on more than twenty planning commissions, committees, and boards, in addition to the directorships of museums and historical agencies.

5. Robert R. Archibald, *The New Town Square: Museums and Communities in Transition* (Walnut Creek, CA: AltaMira Press, 2004), 64.

6. Tapscott and Williams, *Wikinomics*, 247.

7. Duncan Grewcock, "Museums of Cities and Urban Futures: New Approaches to Urban Planning and the Opportunities for Museums of Cities," *Museum International*, no. 231, vol. 58, no. 3 (September 2006): 39–40.

4

"The Novelties of the Town"

Museums, Cities, and Historical Representation

ERIC SANDWEISS

In 2007, representatives of the world's city museums met in Vienna—an apt gathering for the place characterized by Vienna Museum director Wolfgang Kos, several years prior, as a city "in danger of becoming a museum itself."[1] The imbrication of historical memory within the Viennese streetscape, as Kos and others have described it, is neither new nor unintended. The grand boulevard system with which late-nineteenth-century architects, planners, and political leaders sought to modernize the Austrian capital earned its iconic stature not simply by streamlining the flow of traffic and facilitating nearby real estate investment, but through its less quantifiable achievement of appropriating the symbolism of the past to represent the new power of the nation-state. Parliament, university, church, opera, and museum—all partook of the same great conceit, compressing for the Viennese and their provincial subjects a survey of European civilization and its achievements within the length of a single carriage ride across the Austro-Hungarian capital. Today, as visitors take in the same sights through the windows of the No. 1 streetcar, the passage of a century has blurred the novelty of this experiment in architectural borrowing. The entire Ringstrasse presents itself to the casual observer as an undifferentiated display of the charms of "old" Vienna—much as the artistic treasures of Rome, witnessed by an overwhelmed Mark Twain a century earlier, blended together into a "crazy chaos" of Old Masters, a "tempest of pictures" exhausting the bemused traveler with their quantity and variety.[2]

That the Ring and other nineteenth- and early-twentieth-century Western planning innovations made liberal use of historical visual rhetoric (and here one thinks of the carefully coordinated, historically conscious architectural guidelines that accompanied Haussmann's plans for Paris's modern boulevards; of London's Thames Embankment, gracing that city with a classical waterside entry even as it helped to manage a growing sewage problem; of Daniel Burnham's neo-Baroque visions for managing traffic and commerce in Chicago and San Francisco) is one reflection of the ease with which urbanites of that time reconciled, even demanded, history with their modernity. Like central Vienna, such landscapes invite only a vague sense, among today's citizens, of the distinction between the era in which they were crafted and the eras they sought to evoke—a fact that may suggest either success or failure, depending on how one views the goals of early city planners. In either case, however, the reification of history in material fragments, laid sequentially within the urban landscape, reminds us of how much like a procession through the galleries of a museum the experience of a city—not just Vienna—can be.

As it happens, the evolutions of the historical museum and of modern urban planning are not unrelated. The museum occupied a distinct place of interest—right up there with water-treatment facilities and traffic rights-of-way—in the minds of many of the architects and writers who delegated to themselves the task of defining the new planning profession. Yet the question of just what such an institution might do, and of how it might relate to the city around it, was anything but settled in their minds. Fin de siècle Vienna's two great planning visionaries—Otto Wagner and Camillo Sitte—shared little, as historian Carl Schorske mentions, outside the unrealized dream of designing a great museum that might encapsulate their lives' work—and even there, their visions diverged dramatically. Wagner, seeking late in his career to claim ownership of an original, functional approach to architecture, spent more than a decade applying his ideas to the ultimately unsuccessful design of a building for Vienna's Historisches Museum at its new site on the Karlsplatz. It may be that the history museum's strikingly modern design reflected his devotion to that project's historical program less than it did his own ongoing preoccupation with yet another museum proposal, the "Gallery for Artworks of Our Age"—an institution that Wagner proposed to dedicate to the as-yet-unmade art of the coming century, in the process reflecting his own quest to transcend the architectural and planning principles of his earlier career.[3] Sitte's own "Dutchman's Tower" museum, of which Schorske finds only sketchy evidence in the architect's papers, represented a similarly idealized scheme—in this case to construct a building isolated from the distractions of the city, the very fabric of which represented a compendium of the history of art and civilization. Here was a concentrated version of the goals of the shapers of the Ringstrasse, shorn of any pretense of functionality or obligation to serve a larger civic purpose.

Both Sitte's and Wagner's art museum schemes—and, to a lesser extent, Wagner's determinedly original design for the ill-fated city museum project—reflected the fin de siècle avant-garde's restlessness with the sort of eclectic, fragmented historicism that characterized both the late-nineteenth-century city plan and the experience of crowded history museums like Paris's Carnavalet, first conceived in 1866 and opened later in the century.[4] Yet not all city planners had despaired of the goal of linking a city museum, with its obligatory devotion to the past, more directly to a vision of a future urban order.

It was to another sort of tower—less exotic than Sitte's imagined refuge—that Patrick Geddes in 1892 invited Edinburgh residents to learn more about their community and its place in the nation and the world. Geddes's Outlook Tower—which treated visitors to a top-floor, camera obscura view of the city before drawing them downward through successive levels of exhibits highlighting the development of their city, nation, continent, and world—offered one model for harnessing the museum's contemplative and retrospective functions to the planner's more activist role in using facts to shape the community's welfare.[5]

Like his intellectual forebear Geddes, the American planner and essayist Lewis Mumford also saw the city as a dynamic creation; like Geddes, too, he considered the city's most important legacy to be not its landscape of brick and stone but its more generalized role in "enlarg[ing] the scope of all human activities, extending them backwards and forwards in time." Mumford's "city in history" functioned, in essence, as a conveyancer of memory and information. Not surprisingly, then, the problem of the city museum occupied the same level of concern for the American critic as it had for other historically conscious planners before him. Not only is the museum, to Mumford, the "most typical institution of the metropolis," but he adds that "one of the principal functions" of the city itself "is to serve as a museum"—a site where people encounter and learn from others seemingly unlike themselves, where the course of future action becomes clear under the light cast by our growing knowledge of the past.[6]

Mumford knew well, of course, that this container of memory has proved a tool of erasure as well, and that the city might as likely become the seat of civilization's demise as of its salvation. That destructive power, he wrote, has been evidenced not simply in the propensity of urban developers to demolish the physical legacy of the past, but also in their eagerness to do so in the historicist garb of such totalizing schemes as the Haussmann boulevards and Burnham civic centers, which despite their neoclassical garb represented to him a "ruthless overriding of [the city's] historic realities."[7]

The city-as-museum, then, was for Mumford as it was for Geddes not Twain's "crazy chaos" of artifacts (whether accreted over time or refashioned anew, as in Vienna, by ambitious planners and architects), but a less tangible storehouse of memory, a durable stratum of experience upon which to "lay a new foundation for urban life" in times of change and crisis.[8]

And what of the place of the museum itself within this museumlike city? The people who founded and operated the museums that memorialized cities' histories—from the Carnavalet and the London Museum through their American counterparts in sites like New York, Detroit, or Chicago—never comfortably accepted the intrinsic, organic quality of the urban

memory of which Mumford wrote, any more than did the people who designed the urban landscapes of the late-nineteenth- and early-twentieth-
century metropolis. Onto Mumford's open-ended formulation of the city
as a palimpsest of meanings to be revealed or concealed from the shifting
vantage points of a culture in constant transformation, early museum curators felt compelled to make of their cities a posed subject, suitable for
framing and protected from the presumably corrosive forces of time. This
contrived historical memory, different in its nature from Mumford's formulation of the city as a living repository of human experience, has indeed
preserved an image of the past. Yet the act of singling out for preservation
elements of the historical urban landscape and urban experience—whether
in the street or in the gallery—has itself proved instrumental in accelerat-
ing the loss of a deeper sense of "the scope of all human activities," one that
might come through a more thoroughgoing reflection upon the experience
of change and even loss.[9] Today, as museums about cities seek to make
themselves more instrumental to the welfare of their surrounding cities,
they do so burdened by the paradox of an institutional history spent at-
tempting to connect with an urban past by thwarting the dynamic flow of
urban change. Like their counterparts in the planning professions who,
having once sought to protect urban landscapes from the effects of unpre-
dictable change, now work just as diligently to foster it, museum workers
today face the challenge of using the tools honed for one job to complete a
quite different task.

Key to understanding these tools is our ability to uncover the history of
their development. Behind the appearance of plans by such notables as
Wagner, Sitte, or Geddes, behind Mumford's conceptual speculation, lay a
specific history of museums and of their efforts to represent urban order.
This essay considers primarily the trajectory followed by such museums in
the United States. While not entirely separate from their European counterparts, American city museums reflected the particular concerns of a nation seeking to memorialize itself almost before it had developed a history.
As such, the American city museum was especially well poised to join its
mission to that of the men and women who, at virtually the same moment,
shaped the streets and buildings that constituted the elements of its stories.

As museums go, the idea of a building devoted to the display of artifacts related strictly to the historical past—as opposed to artifacts of art or natural history—is not particularly old. It postdates the long tradition of curiosity cabinets, royal galleries, and expositions that constitutes the more general lineage of the modern-day museum. The further notion of focusing the history museum's mission strictly upon a city, rather than on a broader political or geographic terrain, is more recent still. The Carnavalet, first suggested to Prefect of the Seine Georges-Eugène Haussmann as a repository ("*en manière de chapelle expiatoire*") for some of the historical elements pried loose from Paris's streetscape by his improvements, would not open in its current form until 1898, the London Museum, succeeding the earlier Guildhall Museum, in 1912.[10]

The developers of American city museums eventually traced their inspiration, in part, to these two European models. But the American museum also enjoyed a close tie to its longer-lived domestic cousin, the state or local historical society. Most often located in major cities, a number of historical societies turned their attention from national or state-specific issues to those of the urban milieu at precisely the time that government officials, social scientists, and architects began conceiving of the city as a meaningful (and problematic) unit of American society. Their decisions to do so— and to do so through museum display rather than through other interpretive media—came relatively late in the development of such institutions; once decided on, their efforts never achieved anywhere near the same effect upon the city as the efforts of those whose historical work took place in the landscape itself.[11]

From the earliest days of independence, Americans' concern to preserve their collective history very nearly outpaced history itself. In 1790, New Yorker John Pintard established a display of artifacts in City Hall; a decade later, control of the nascent collection, by now known as the American Museum, passed to John Scudder. Pintard, meanwhile, led a group of prominent New Yorkers in 1804 to establish a historical institution of a more permanent sort. Constituting themselves the New-York Historical Society, the group called on fellow citizens to join in a search for records that might recover the details of a past already imperiled, they thought, by "ingenious conjectures and amusing fables." The cause of providing a formal venue for the preservation of urban memory proved once again tenuous in its appeal. The most significant reply to the New-York Historical Society's initial public notice came not from collectors, but from the writer Washington Irving, whose *History of New York, from the Beginning of the World to the End of the Dutch Dynasty,* narrated by a fictional curmudgeon named Diedrich Knickerbocker, offered a volume-ful of amusing fables in response. The novelist was, no doubt, gratified to hear DeWitt Clinton, mayor of the city and one of the founders of the new historical society, denounce his "unnatural combination of fiction and history" as being "disgusting to good taste." Clinton's scorn meant that Irving's satiric point had been taken.[12]

Still, the elderly Knickerbocker, stuffing his pockets full of the useless minutiae of his city's past, proved an apt caricature of Clinton and others who followed in his footsteps. The effort "to collect and preserve," as the organization's charter put it, "whatever may relate to the natural, civil, or ecclesiastical History of the United States in general and of this state in particular" represented as focused a mission as early historical societies cared to articulate.[13]

As settlement spread west, a growing number of these societies appeared in cities with histories shallower than those of such early republican centers as Boston, New York, and Philadelphia. In one case after another, their notion of just who should partake of their activities proved as narrow as the scope of their missions was wide. William Barry, elected the first secretary of the Chicago Historical Society in 1857, described his colleagues as "fit, though few," comprising a selection of "our oldest, most respected citizens"; Barry warned soon thereafter that only a "compact and harmonious" organization would resist the "popular excitement" that seemed, to a careful Whig such as himself, as dangerous to good history as it was to good governance. In Saint Louis, a self-described group of "old residents . . . who have spent the flower of their lives in advancing [the city's] interest" met in the county courthouse in 1866 "for the purpose of saving from oblivion the early history of our city and our state"—a meeting that resulted in the establishment of the Missouri Historical Society.

As such "old residents" diminished in number, the stakes of their success seemed to grow higher. In the same year, New-York Historical Society director Frederic de Peyster warned that his city's growing ranks of immigrants "exposed [New York] to the vices of the great cities abroad." De Peyster set a high bar for a historical society, contending that "to counteract the evils, which irreligion, folly and wickedness have thus transplanted, it becomes our duty to control their effects, and then eradicate them, by . . . stem[ming] this flood and mak[ing] it subservient to . . . social progress." Across America, then, these Knickerbockers set a tone for historical societies—particularly big-city societies—that has persisted, in some cases, to our own time. They represented their own interests, their own memories, as those of the city, and left little room for anyone to argue otherwise. In the name of "social progress," they gathered up every bit of evidence that might reflect (or justify) their ascendance to power.[14]

Material progress, on the other hand—reflected more readily in the landscape itself than in the halls of the museum—coexisted uneasily with the founders' original goals. History museums owed their existence to the profits earned on things scraped from the earth, melted in furnaces, heaped on trains, slashed under blades. But such material processes had also caused the effacement of landscape and of memory that made those societies seem necessary in the first place. Rather than memorialize urban progress through display of its physical traces, the early groups typically stressed their moral rise above the commercial realm. "It would be unworthy of the spirit of historical Chicago," wrote the Chicago Historical Society's president in 1882 in campaigning for a new building, "that it should have nothing to show for the future but piles of boxes and bales. . . . There should be some fitting memorial, in no way connected with trade . . . which shall not be touched by the spirit of profit or dividend." The president of the Missouri Historical Society, George Leighton, wrote the following year of his desire for a "philosophical history" of Saint Louis, one that went beyond "the mere compilation of commercial and manufacturing statistics."[15]

And yet the spirit of accumulation underlay the impulse to preserving memory, just as it had the impulse to wealth. An observer of the young

Chicago Historical Society justified that institution's mission with the observation that "our generalizations, our theories, are right in proportion to
the comprehensiveness of the mass of facts from which they are deduced."[16]

It was through amassment of the printed word, then—not of "boxes and
bales"—that the early societies sought to anchor and to regulate memory
in the changing city. (Significantly, the area in which they did evince a consistent interest in museum collecting and exhibition was in the area of
"aboriginal"—that is, preliterate—culture, for which no accompanying
narrative existed. This "cabinet" of prehistoric relics, as the museum arm
was usually known, was solely an adjunct to the larger archiving function
that seemed to the founders so urgent; in fact, as of the late 1700s, the term
"museum" referred as much to magazines as it did to buildings.[17]) Although historical societies' collections soon grew to include more historical urban artifacts, their buildings long remained, in essence, decorated
reading rooms. Typically, the director's position at the New-York Historical
Society continued to be listed as "librarian" until the 1930s. For these
groups, collection and care of the documentary record was the key to holding onto a coherent vision of a more orderly past, one unimpeded by in-
terference from the material vicissitudes of the city itself.

The move to eschew physical display as a means of imparting historical
information reflected scholarly attitudes toward the museum generally. By
the 1860s, museums had acquired something of a tarnished reputation in
the United States—in part because of their place in the shifting urban landscape that historical societies sought to rise above. P. T. Barnum's American
Museum, located in downtown Manhattan until its destruction by fire in
1865, exemplified the blurry distinction between museum-as-entertainment
and museum-as-education. Yet in terms of practical collecting strategies,
relatively little distance separated Barnum, searching the country for "albi-
noes, fat boys, giants, [and] dwarfs," from Philadelphia's Charles Willson
Peale, keeper of the nation's best-known early museum, and his desire to
present "rational amusements" in the service of revealing "divine wisdom."
In fact, Peale's collection itself was partially absorbed by Barnum in his
continuing quest for more objects. So, too, was John Scudder's original
American Museum, which lent its name as well as its actual collections to

Barnum's showplace. In Cincinnati and in Saint Louis, wherever urbanization led in the antebellum decades, new "museums" promised the curious
public mastodon bones beside three-dimensional re-creations of Hell,
mermaids next to arrowheads. Sensation—exposure to "the world in
miniature" as Peale had sought—never stood far from sensationalism, Barnum's "superfluity of novelties." What they shared was precisely what the
early societies sought to avoid: a reliance on things to trigger a more immediate form of understanding—revelation, not cerebration; emotion, not
distance.[18]

A superfluity of novelties, of course, was what the city itself offered. Barnum, in a manner that Lewis Mumford himself might have appreciated,
saw his own operation as exemplary of "the novelties of the town"; an experience of the kind that country people couldn't see elsewhere. Indeed,
others noted the link too, although they framed it in less positive terms. A
modern reader cannot help but be struck by the mounting criticisms of the
opacity and disorder of the urban landscape, and the ways in which civic
and intellectual leaders saw the contents of the museums themselves. The
Smithsonian Institution's pioneering curator, George Brown Goode, criti-
cized the typical history museum as a "chance assemblage of curiosities,"
while various observers sniped that the belongings of the New-York Historical Society were "distributed about in dark corridors," or that the
Chicago Historical Society's collections were "cheap and cheerless" and
"full of queer old things." Missouri Historical Society, after only seven years
of existence, was judged to be "nearly as much of a fossil as the specimens
which crowd its cabinets." Such language matched the concern of late-nineteenth-century urban observers like Jacob Riis, Frederick Law Olmsted,
and Charles Mulford Robinson for the "sunless and joyless streets" of the
ostensibly chaotic city that they sought to reform and re-form, outside of
the museum's walls.[19]

Just as American civic officials began to employ the services of Olmsted,
Robinson, George Kessler, John Nolen, and others to reorganize the physical layouts of their streets and parks, historical society boards (often comprising the same people) began to expand and systematize their artifactual
collections. From the 1880s on, the once-incidental cabinets, or museums,

were reconceived as transparent interior landscapes, readable and reliable contrasts to the difficult world of the street. The objects within them, conjoined with appropriate textual documentation, were presented as the agents of instruction rather than of mere sensation. The museum of the future would, in Goode's words, constitute "a collection of instructive labels each illustrated by a well-selected specimen." If objects were indeed a part of the historical society's purview, they would be put to the service of ideas; the museum would become a classroom, not a laboratory. This controlling urge was complemented by the decision of a number of organizations to push toward their long-held goals of erecting buildings that might themselves serve as instructive objects. The lure of a prominent place in the landscape of "city beautiful" clearly appealed to the keepers of the still largely marginal historical societies. From within the dim chambers of their downtown libraries, they had sought unsuccessfully to tie the perceived importance of their collections to a proportionate level of influence upon the surrounding city. Their new civic monuments, rising along the edges of large public parks far from the business district (at the same time as Otto Wagner was erecting his working model of the facade of Vienna's history museum in the Karlsplatz), constituted architectural artifacts whose scale surpassed not only that of the collections housed within, but also of the surrounding streets.[20]

But even as the colonnades were rising along parkways and boulevards, historical societies continued to suffer from public protests of the futility of seeking to capture a meaningful memory of something as dynamic as the modern city—either in their libraries (often parodied as sleeping lounges for aging capitalists), their tedious lecture series ("gaseous secretions of vanity and dilettantism," to the New York diarist George Templeton Strong), or their long rows of glass cases. Again, the city had outpaced its chroniclers' ability to make sense of what they saw. Across the disciplines of American intellectual culture in the 1890s, while city-history museums invested heavily in the taxonomic model of explanation, others had begun to conceive of the city as a more strictly social phenomenon, to make of its protean quality a positive thing, not a danger. The economist Adna Weber, one of the first of the master theorists of urban culture, had tried to sum up the importance of nineteenth-century cities in terms of their role as the incubators of "a broader and freer judgment and a great inclination to and appreciation of new thoughts, manners, and ideals." Others, including George Herbert Mead and John Dewey, were framing their new concepts of selfhood in social terms, finding in the city the ultimate laboratory for human interchange at its most complex. Such ideas only cast harsher light on the problem of how to memorialize the dynamism of the city within the museum, which by its nature honored the concrete over the abstract, the constant over the changing.[21]

The suggestions for integrating historical representation with a more active program of social engagement appeared in fits and starts. Geddes's plans for Edinburgh have already been mentioned. Americans were not far behind. "Why confine the aim of the society," wrote a *New York Times* editorialist of that city's historical society in the 1890s, "to the comparatively narrow object of historical research?" In place of the society's plans for a new showcase on Central Park West, the author suggested a "museum for artisans"—a building open in a site, and at times convenient to working-class New Yorkers, a place where they might investigate the beauty and importance of their own lives, rather than be reminded of their own relative insignificance. In 1903, the influential librarian John Cotton Dana proposed that the "chief concern" of urban cultural institutions like libraries was "the process, not the product, of education," and that they ought to be seen as sites primarily "for diffusing sound principles of social and political action."[22]

The populist turn affected even the stuffiest of the historical organizations. Chicago, the society that had once bragged of its "fit, though few" members, dedicated its new building in 1896 not to "any sect or clique," but "to [the] benefit of the whole community." A generation later, the Chicago Historical Society moved yet again, this time to its current Georgian quarters at the southern edge of Lincoln Park. With the move, the institution sought to reform at one stroke its architectural image, the content of its collections, and the manner of their display. In turning from the previously popular stylistic language of the classical revival to the more domesticated Georgian, or colonial revival, they identified themselves as one of a growing breed of museums, like the Museum of the City of New York, established across Central Park from the more exclusive New-York Historical Society—aspiring to a more accessible image within the city. The Chicago Historical Society bought the vast estate of a local confectioner named Charles Gunther, who had operated his own museum of curiosities above his State Street candy store—including the mummy of Moses's mother and the original serpent of the Garden of Eden—and who had once taken down, brick by brick, the Confederate Libby Prison from its site in Richmond, Virginia, and reconstructed it as a tourist attraction on Chicago's South Side. In installing these and other collections in dioramas and re-created period rooms, the museum joined a growing number of similar institutions seeking to replace entirely the now ill-favored method of taxonomic display with a more emotive, more all-encompassing form of display, one that made of the viewer an ostensible participant in, rather than critic of the past. "An antidote for the prevalent movie habit," gushed a local arts critic of the new museum, while another journalist praised the Chicago Historical Society for "breathing new life into its collections" by removing its "relics" from their "dreary glass cases." Not long after, in Detroit, a "Streets of Detroit" exhibition, carefully separated from the real streets of Detroit by a new, windowless modernist museum structure on Woodward Avenue, provided a similar thrill to citizens whose only previous local-history museum experiences had taken place in a suite of rooms, crowded with shelves and cases, tucked away on a high floor of a downtown skyscraper.[23]

But the upbeat suggestions of "breathing new life," the hopeful comparisons to moviegoing, also pointed to the continuing problem of conceiving of the historical society as the repository of urban memory. If verisimilitude was what they now sought, museums could never possibly keep up with movies and radio, let alone with reality. In cities across the country, local groups had already begun the practice of erecting plaques on historic buildings, framing the street itself as a museum-like experience. In Williamsburg, Virginia, and in Dearborn, Michigan, the era's great capitalists, Rockefeller and Ford, were busy investing their millions in the full-scale renovation or re-creation of entire buildings. Meanwhile, in Charleston, South Carolina; Santa Fe, New Mexico; and New Orleans,

Louisiana, the new legal tool of historic district zoning made outdoor museums of entire urban districts. Such efforts increasingly framed the urban landscape itself within historical reference points. The American city, long resistant to the kind of centralized planning that had encased the improvements of London, Paris, and Vienna in their historicist wrappings, at last began to reflect a more systematic appropriation of historical imagery for the purposes of modern improvement.[24]

American museums sought to respond to the challenge in a manner that shored up their authority in opposition to the blandishments of the street. By the 1970s, many had returned to Goode's century-old preference for "instructive labels illustrated by well-selected specimens"—a trend encouraged, in this case, by calls for greater inclusivity and social-historical rigor. Asked in 1992 about his approach to exhibitions, Ellsworth Brown, then director of the Chicago Historical Society, stated that "exhibitions should be about ideas." Rick Beard, then of the Museum of the City of New York, explained that he began the process by "creating . . . a very long monograph with appropriate scholarly apparatus, bibliography, and some notes, and our interpretations come from that document for the various media we employ."[25] Such thinking was encouraged, in material ways, by the criteria of one of the most important funding agencies for museum exhibitions, the National Endowment for the Humanities (NEH).

NEH standards indeed imparted a measure of intellectual discipline to many exhibitions. But in allowing such criteria, inadvertently, to short-change the medium of their craft for its message, many museum professionals laid aside Peale's and Barnum's simple insight into the stimulating effect of seeing the "world in miniature." They rejected "the novelties of the town"—the vivid if unreliable evidence of the past that, as Mumford saw it, permeates the urban landscape—in favor of their earliest predecessors' distrust of unmediated sensation. That the narratives of idea-driven exhibits focused more on the once-forgotten, or excluded, than on the familiar denizens of corporate boardrooms or society blue books does not change the fact that they were usually developed by staff and consultants who, if forced, would still have to describe themselves as "fit though few."

Figures within the very landscapes that they purport to represent, city museums had come to seem time-bound, historical artifacts in their own right. In their initial efforts at amassing written records toward the end of reconstructing accurately and completely an imagined civic unity, and in their subsequent attempts to re-create the dynamism of the landscape itself, they had offered two models for "extending [human activity] . . . forward in time." Neither proved particularly successful in garnering public credibility and acceptance. The former tendency, echoed in the late-twentieth-century turn back toward a more intellectual approach to historical interpretation, suffered from a general disenchantment over monadic historical interpretation. The latter, meanwhile, could only suffer from comparison to what landscape historian Denis Cosgrove has termed "the ever more seamless elision of experience and landscape" that characterizes our own time.[26]

What remains, then, for the city museum of today, equipped as it is with tools designed for other jobs at other times—tools that worked only sporadically even then? The representational city is realized less effectively, today, within museum walls than it is through large-scale historic preservation projects, in consumption-oriented spaces, or in the verisimilitude of film and electronic media—all of which have more powerfully influenced our collective memory of the urban past.[27] Instead of overtly rejecting the past, modern planners have done Vienna's Ringstrasse (now part of a UNESCO World Heritage site) one better: placing a comfortable, commodified frame of memory around the city and the world. Under the guise of expanded access to historical information, we inhabit a world managed by ever fewer producers, fewer interpreters, fewer true alternatives to the comfortable habits that we fashioned so successfully from the labors of our predecessors. Life itself seems as though it were set within a museum or upon a stage—a seeming rush of color, noise, experience that actually plays itself out in well-packaged, well-sponsored segments.

Just as the deceptive historicism of grand boulevards and pedimented public buildings helped to send Sitte, Wagner, and others in search of a museum somehow purified of the influences of surrounding mediations of the past, today's well-framed urban landscape demands its own response from those who would seek to represent the city from a critical perspective. As history has become its own sort of product, a modern-day equivalent of the "boxes and bales" above which cultural leaders once sought to rise, museums about cities are left high and dry, working to compete in a larger marketplace of images and artifacts. The conveners of the meeting at Vienna in 2007 shared a range of ideas and plans for ways in which the once-sanctified walls of their museums might soon shelter and nourish the more truly endangered aspects of the contemporary city: change, unpredictability, and social fluidity—in short, the "novelties of the town." These forces, all of which once seemed to threaten our ability to connect urban past to urban future, now stand in danger of becoming historical artifacts in their own right.

NOTES

Portions of this chapter appeared previously as Eric Sandweiss, "Framing Urban Memory: The Changing Role of History Museums in the American City," in *Memory and Architecture*, ed. Eleni Bastea (Albuquerque: University of New Mexico Press, 2004), 25–48.

1. Wolfgang Kos, "Old Vienna, the City That Never Was: An Exhibition to Discuss the Identity of a City," in *City Museums as Centres of Civic Dialogue? Proceedings of the Fourth Conference of the International Association of City Museums, Amsterdam, 3–5 November 2005*, ed. Renée Kistemaker (Amsterdam: Amsterdam Historical Museum, 2006), 154.

2. Mark Twain, *The Innocents Abroad, or the New Pilgrims' Progress*, vol. 2 (New York: Harper and Brothers, 1906), 15.

3. Peter Haiko, "The Franz Josef-Stadtmuseum: The Attempt to Implement a Theory of Modern Architecture," in *Otto Wagner: Reflections on the Raiment of Modernity*, ed. Harry Francis Mallgrave (Santa Monica, CA: Getty Center for the History of Art and the Humanities, 1993), 52–83; Carl E. Schorske, *Fin-de-Siècle Vienna: Politics and Culture* (New York: Vintage Books, 1981), 105–110; Andrew Kincaid, "Memory and the City: Urban Renewal and Literary Memoirs in Contemporary Dublin," *College Literature* 32, no. 2 (2005): 19–20.

4. Georges Cain, "Le Musée Carnavalet," *Figaro Illustré,* April 1909, 6; Karl Baedeker, *Paris and Environs, with Routes from London to Paris: Handbook for Travelers,* 11th ed. (London, 1894), 210–212.

5. Jordanna Bailkin, "Radical Conservations: The Problem with the London Museum," *Radical History Review* 84 (2002): 47; Chas. Zueblin, "The World's First Sociological Laboratory," *American Journal of Sociology* 4, no. 5 (March 1899): 577–592; Joyce Earley, "Sorting in Patrick Geddes' Outlook Tower," *Places* 7, no. 3 (1991): 63–71.

6. Lewis Mumford, *The City in History: Its Origins, Its Transformations, and Its Prospects* (New York: Harcourt, Brace, & World, 1961), 561–562.

7. Mumford, *The City in History,* 402.

8. Mumford, *The City in History,* 569, 3.

9. The critical literature on preservation and its problematic relation to history and memory is large and continues to grow. Among the many works useful in the preparation of this study, see M. Christine Boyer, *The City of Collective Memory: Its Historical Imagery and Architectural Entertainments* (Cambridge: MIT Press, 1994); David Lowenthal, *Possessed by the Past: The Heritage Crusade and the Spoils of History* (New York: Free Press, 1996); Françoise Choay, *The Invention of the Historic Monument* (New York: Cambridge University Press, 2001); Larry Bennett, *Fragments of Cities: The New American Downtowns and Neighborhoods* (Columbus: Ohio State University Press, 1990); Dolores Hayden, *The Power of Place: Urban Landscapes as Public History* (Cambridge: MIT Press, 1995); Max Page, *The Creative Destruction of Manhattan, 1900–1940* (Chicago: University of Chicago Press, 1999). On the development of professional standards of historical objectivity see Peter Novick, *That Noble Dream: The Objectivity Question and the American Historical Profession* (Cambridge, UK: Cambridge University Press, 1988). On commemoration and the construction of public memory within the United States, see Michael Kammen, *Mystic Chords of Memory: The Transformation of Tradition in American Culture* (New York: Knopf, 1991), and John Bodnar, *Remaking America: Public Memory, Commemoration, and Patriotism in the Twentieth Century* (Princeton, NJ: Princeton University Press, 1992).

10. Cain, "Le Musée Carnavalet," 6; Francis Sheppard, *The Treasury of London's Past: An Historical Account of the Museum of London and Its Predecessors, the Guildhall Museum and the London Museum* (London: HMSO Books, 1991), 39.

11. On early historical societies, see Walter Muir Whitehill, *Independent Historical Societies: An Enquiry into Their Research and Publication Functions and Their Financial Future* (Boston: The Atheneum, 1962), and Julian P. Boyd, "State and Local Historical Societies in the United States," *American Historical Review* 40, no. 1 (1934): 10–37.

12. On New-York Historical Society generally, see R. W. G. Vail, *Knickerbocker Birthday: A Sesquicentennial History of the New-York Historical Society, 1804–1954* (New York: New-York Historical Society Press, 1954), and Pamela Spence Richards, *Scholars and Gentlemen: The Library of the New-York Historical Society, 1804–1982* (Hamden, CT: Archon Books, 1984). See also Washington Irving, *A History of New York, from the Beginning of the World to the End of the Dutch Dynasty* (New York: A. L. Burt, c. 1848). Clinton quoted in Mary Weatherspoon Bowden, "Knickerbocker's *History* and the 'Enlightened Men of New York City,'" *American Literature* 47, no. 2 (1975): 159.

13. Vail, *Knickerbocker Birthday*, 23.

14. "Fit though few": William Barry to L. A. Lapham, April 29, 1856, Folder 1, William Barry Papers, Chicago Historical Society Archives; "compact and harmonious," cited in Paul M. Angle, *The Chicago Historical Society, 1856–1956: An Unconventional Chronicle* (New York: Rand McNally, 1956), 23; "old residents": public notice, Aug. 1, 1866, included in *Missouri Historical Society Collections* 1, no. 1 (n.d.): 25; "saving from oblivion": "The Origin of the Missouri Historical Society," *The Invincible Magazine* 1, no. 1 (1913): 9; Frederic de Peyster, *The Moral and Intellectual Influence of Libraries upon Social Progress* (New York: New-York Historical Society, 1866), 48.

15. *Historical Chicago: Past, Present, and Future: Address of Emery A. Storrs for the Benefit of the Chicago Historical Society* (Chicago, 1882), 10; George Leighton, "Annual Address of the President, January 16, 1883," *Missouri Historical Society Collections* 1, no. 7 (1883): 10–11.

16. *Chicago Tribune*, February 9, 1865.

17. See among many similar titles in the late 1700s, *The Massachusetts Magazine, or, Monthly Museum of Knowledge and Rational Entertainment* (1789–1796).

18. P. T. Barnum, *Struggles and Triumphs, or Forty Years' Recollections* (1989; New York: Penguin, 1987), 103; Peale cited in Neil Harris, *Humbug: The Art of P. T.*

Barnum (Boston: Little-Brown, 1973), 34, and David R. Brigham, *Public Culture in the Early Republic: Peale's Museum and Its Audience* (Washington, DC: Smithsonian Institution Press, 1995), 20–21; Peale-Pintard-Barnum connection, see Barnum, *Struggles and Triumphs*, 101–102, and John Rickards Betts, "P. T. Barnum and the Popularization of Natural History," *Journal of the History of Ideas* 20, no. 3 (June–September 1959), 353–368; M. H. Dunlop, "Curiosities Too Numerous to Mention: Early Regionalism and Cincinnati's Western Museum," *American Quarterly* 36, no. 4 (Fall 1984): 524–548; John F. McDermott, "Museums in Early St. Louis," *Bulletin of the Missouri Historical Society* 4, no. 3 (April 1948): 30ff.

19. Barnum, *Struggles and Triumphs*, 136; Goode cited in Archie F. Key, *Beyond Four Walls: The Origin and Development of Canadian Museums* (Toronto: McClelland and Stewart, 1973), 91; New-York Historical Society: *New York Evening Post*, December 26, 1884, cited in Vail, *Knickerbocker Birthday*, 157; Chicago Historical Society: *Chicago Herald*, June 20, 1886, cited in Angle, *Chicago Historical Society*, 118; Missouri Historical Society: W. H. H. Russell, "The Missouri Historical Society," *Central Magazine* 3, no. 1 (July 1873): 417; Jacob A. Riis, *How the Other Half Lives: Studies among the Tenements of New York* (New York: Scribner, 1890), 33.

20. Goode cited in Kenneth Hudson, *A Social History of Museums: What the Visitors Thought* (London: Macmillan, 1975), 68; William H. Wilson, *The City Beautiful Movement* (Baltimore: Johns Hopkins University Press, 1989). Typical of the monumental cultural institutions erected in the late 1800s and early 1900s were the structures of the museums examined in this study, including the New-York Historical Society (1906), Museum of the City of New York (1932), Chicago Historical Society (1896, with another new building in 1932), and Missouri Historical Society (1915).

21. Strong cited in Vail, *Knickerbocker Birthday*, 114; Adna Ferrin Weber, *The Growth of Cities in the Nineteenth Century: A Study in Statistics* (New York, Macmillan, 1899), 432–434; George Herbert Mead, *Mind, Self, and Society: From the Standpoint of a Behaviorist*, ed. Charles W. Morris (Chicago: University of Chicago Press, 1934); John Dewey, *Democracy and Education: An Introduction to the Philosophy of Education* (New York: Macmillan, 1926).

22. "A Museum for Artisans," *New York Times*, April 24, 1892; John Cotton Dana, *A Library Primer*, 3rd ed. (Chicago: Little-Brown, 1903), 13.

23. "Sect or clique" cited in Angle, *Chicago Historical Society*, 137; on the Lincoln Park building see Angle, *Chicago Historical Society*, 195ff.; on MCNY see "'A Vanished City Is Restored': Inventing and Displaying the Past at the Museum of the City of New York," chapter 5 in Page, *Creative Destruction*; on Gunther's museum see Clement Silvestro, "The Candy Man's Mixed Bag," *Chicago History* 2, no. 2 (Fall 1972): 86–99, as well as Gunther Scrapbook, Chicago Historical Society Archives; "breathing new life": *Dallas News*, October 20, 1938, cited in Angle, *Chicago Historical Society*, 214; on Detroit, see Henry D. Brown, "Our New Museum: A Building—A Program," *Bulletin of the Detroit Historical Society* 9 (May 1949): 5–12.

24. On Williamsburg and Greenfield Village, see Michael Wallace, "History Museums in the United States," in *Presenting the Past*, ed. Susan Porter Benson, Stephen Brier, and Roy Rosenzweig (Philadelphia: Temple University Press, 1986). On New Orleans, see "Invented Traditions and Cityscapes," in Boyer, *City of Collective Memory*, chap. 6; on Santa Fe, see Chris Wilson, *The Myth of Santa Fe: Creating a Modern Regional Tradition* (Albuquerque: University of New Mexico Press, 1997).

25. Bruce M. Stave, "A Conversation with Ellsworth Brown," *Journal of Urban History* 18, no. 4 (1992): 479; Bruce M. Stave, "A Conversation with Rick Beard," *Journal of Urban History* 23, no. 5 (1997): 204.

26. Denis E. Cosgrove, *Social Formation and Symbolic Landscape* (Madison: University of Wisconsin Press, 1998), xxiv.

27. See Michael Sorkin, ed., *Variations on a Theme Park: The New American City and the End of Public Space* (New York: Hill and Wang, 1997).

5

The Prospect of a City Museum

JACK LOHMAN

Let's take Dublin, capital of the Irish Republic. Raphael Holinshed's *Chronicles* of 1577, a ragtag Tudor history of the British Isles, includes a fascinating essay called "The Description of Ireland," by Richard Stanyhurst. He describes Dublin, the city of his birth, with all the enthusiasm of a Tudor tourist brochure:

> This citie, *as* it is not in antiquitie inferiour to anie citie in Ireland, *so* in pleasant situation, in gorgious buildings, in the multitude of the people, in martiall chivalrie, in obedience and loialtie, in the abundance of wealth, in largenesse of hospitalite, in maners and civilitie *it is* superiour to all other cities and townes in that realme. And therefore it is commonlie called the Irish, or yoong, London.[1]

Stanyhurst names this Irish London "the beautie and eie of Ireland."[2] It's a striking phrase, and one that gathers up everything from "gorgious buildings" to the city's pleasing "situation" to the "hospitality, manners, and civility" of its citizens.

And such a capacious view of the city, of its meaning and culture, is significant. If we are to picture the importance of any city nationally and on the world stage, we must use the widest lens possible to ensure that we leave nothing out. If we are to tell the story of a metropolis such as London or Paris or Dublin—as of course Stanyhurst himself is doing in his fashion— we need to consider every aspect of its urban personality.

City museums—those repositories of good intention—formalize such stories. They take the worthy past and try at the very least to hold on to it and, at best, to recapture it for today's citizens. But it's a risky business. If cities are viewed too narrowly, such museums can easily become mausoleums, a late attempt to capture something that has already happened, which has already gone. The grandfatherly sigh of "the olde days" falls heavily from each bit of text mounted on a wall or dusty display case— dreary for the best of us, fatal for the YouTube generation. Why is it that city museums often seem as if the city had departed?

It is essential, therefore, before we come to the question of what sort of institution we might want to represent a city, that we first understand what sort of a city it is that we wish to celebrate.

BUILT ENVIRONMENT: "GORGEOUS BUILDINGS"

It sometimes seems as if two contrary principles are at play in cities. One wants to tear things down, to start over, to improve the decayed with the new. Cities, the progressivists argue, are about life, about renovation, about the living —and need to be made better.

Their opponents struggle to hold on to the past. They insist that the visionaries of renewal must understand the importance of what went before. Proponents of historical culture argue that we are nourished by the past, not just burdened by its lack of underfloor heating.

The urban planning pioneer Patrick Geddes worked in Dublin from 1911 to 1914. Like all town planners, Geddes was interested in how cities worked. He had a particular fascination with communications, with the city as a network of interconnecting functions.

But Geddes was no crass utilitarian and was international in his approach. In his work in India, he quickly realized that neoclassical notions of order were certainly not the only principles of reasoned architecture and civic unity—though his colonial superiors, keen to establish the symbolic structures of their rule, tried to convince him otherwise. Unlike most of his peers, Geddes found (as one architectural historian has described it) beauty in the ragged tangles of the old towns, the narrow twisted lanes with earthen dwellings and the main streets with stylish buildings that formed what Geddes could see was "an inseparably interwoven structure." The seeming chaos that colonial administrators sought to remove (and, if we're honest, feared) was of their own imagining—the product of a Western addiction to mechanical order. What Geddes perceived was something he called "the order of life in development."[3]

I raise this sense of urban chaos to begin a list of qualities one might wish to see in a museum about a city. You can hardly get away from "the order of life" in a city as crowded and bustling as London, but it is exactly the quality one needs to hold onto in any city museum.

Geddes saw this clearly in terms of building successful cities, not just in India, but in Europe. His most celebrated book on town planning, *Cities in Evolution,* was published in 1914, at the end of his time in Dublin. In it, he wrote:

> Above all things, [we must] seek to enter into the spirit of our city, its historical essence and continuous life. . . . Its civic character—its collective soul, thus in some measure discerned and entered into—its daily life—may then be more fully touched.[4]

To understand what is there already is to see the great resource on which a museum about a city can build. It may be the busiest public square where street performers jostle with businesspeople on a sunny day, or the traffic roaring through the streets. But it may equally encompass great buildings such as the Louvre, Beijing's Temple of Heaven, Sydney's Opera House, or, on a more modest scale, Berlin's Brandenburg Gate or Dublin's Custom House. These too are important, for they can convey a sense of a city's ambitions, of its sense of itself as a city. In 1799, one writer called the Custom House "the most sumptuous edifice appropriate to such a use in Europe,"[5] and we mustn't forget the scale of such an achievement.

The point, as Geddes understood, is that the city's culture is already present: It exists, both as a living past that can be explained now, and as a thriving presence in the city's cultural capital. "Civic character," as Geddes calls it, is in the air, and any city museum worth its salt must never try to restrict that character by boxing it into narrow display cases called "Dublin in the Eighteenth Century" or "Shanghai Today." It must establish a living connection with the past and present environments that are all around us. It must draw power from the thriving city life we feel the very moment we step onto the streets.

LANDSCAPE: "PLEASANT SITUATION"

There is an aspect to the city that is not the city at all. If you ask most people about London, their first description is of monuments—Big Ben, the Tower of London, St. Paul's Cathedral—"gorgeous buildings" of the kind that struck Richard Stanyhurst in his paean to Dublin.

But Stanyhurst recognized that cities, those fabrications of bricks and mortar, are not just marked by their most obvious difference from the countryside. Great cities share something of the beauty of their landscape. Great cities have, in Stanyhurst's phrase, a "pleasant situation." And he finds Dublin, of course, a place not just of beauty, but of a kind of pleasing moderation:

> The seat of this citie is of all sides pleasant, comfortable, and wholesome. If you would traverse hils, they are not far off. If champion ground, it lieth of all parts. If you be delited with fresh water, the famous river called the *Liffie*, named of Ptolomé *Lybnium*, runneth fast by. If you will take the view of the sea, it is at hand.[6]

If we are happy with that, why bother visiting a museum at all? But let's raise the stakes.

The river is a key feature of London's history as it is of so many cities, from the first Roman settlement along the Thames bringing trade and commerce from the Mediterranean and North Africa, to nineteenth-century communities of Chinese immigrants building one of London's many "small cities" in Limehouse in the city's docklands area.

Poets from Spenser to Ben Okri have sung the blandishments of the "sweet Thames" for centuries. But is this how people *experience* the river—or any part of the urban setting? To get closer to the spirit of the city, we need a keener eye. Here is Charles Dickens, for instance, in the celebrated opening passage to *Bleak House:*

> Fog everywhere. Fog up the river, where it flows among green aits and meadows; fog down the river, where it rolls defiled among the tiers of shipping and the waterside pollutions of a great (and dirty) city. Fog on the Essex marshes, fog on the Kentish heights. Fog creeping into the cabooses of collier-brigs; fog lying out on the yards, and hovering in the rigging of great ships; fog drooping on the gunwales of barges and small boats. Fog in the eyes and throats of ancient Greenwich pensioners, wheezing by the firesides of their wards; fog in the stem and bowl of the afternoon pipe of the wrathful skipper, down in his close cabin; fog cruelly pinching the toes and fingers of his shivering little 'prentice boy on deck.[7]

You can feel in Dickens's language the great benighted course of the Thames rolling beneath the foggy air of Victorian London. Here is the city; here is what the past felt like. Not pretty, not placid—but something real and alive. We all know what happens if you go down to the river . . .

If the Museum of London can get this feeling across, then it is doing one of its jobs, which is to convey to twenty-first-century visitors what it was like to be a Londoner in the past.

LONDONERS, DUBLINERS: "MANNERS AND CIVILITY"
London lost hold of its river for a while with the decline of the docks and boat traffic, and is only just beginning to reclaim it as a space of leisure, of walkways and cafés and social mix. The spectacular views from the London Eye, the large Ferris wheel on the south bank of the Thames, have played their part, as has global warming—though it is likely that the Charles Dickenses of the twenty-first century will not be writing so much about the pervasive fog, which has long since disappeared, as about floods, spilling over from the Kentish heights to the Essex marshes.

Cultural capitals have their famous buildings, their celebrated rivers and hills. But of course it is the people of the city who are to a large extent what interests visitors to any city museum. To convey *vividly* a sense of the past is to describe how the city was lived in, where people went, what they did—

to find social behaviors analogous to our own lifestyles (as we would now call them) today.

Thinking of a sunny walk along the Thames in London, one can imagine the qualities of urban existence that one knows visitors to the Museum of London would relate to: the leisurely pace, the beautiful views, the social variety one encounters.

To take Dublin as our "Irish London," we can draw on a similar sense of what we might call historic leisure. Dublin's famous pleasure grounds in the eighteenth century were the Beaux' Walk on St. Stephen's Green, and Gardiner's Mall in what is now O'Connell Street. Situated on either side of the river, they competed for the patronage of the fashionable crowd. Who went there? According to a French visitor in 1796, "worthy mothers were thin on the ground, and seemed worried. Young ladies, on the other hand, were very numerous and seemed happily occupied. . . ."[8]

Contemporary engravings of these pleasure gardens exist, and yes, one can mount them on the wall and say, "Look. This is what Dublin was like in the past." But how much more do we need the suspicious gaze of our French tourist monitoring—or is he ogling, really?—the amorous young ladies of Dublin. How much more do we need to know that the north side rival to the Beaux' Walk was built as a speculative property development by the Gardiner family, who were hoping to draw on the success of St. Stephen's Green south of the river.[9] A similar experience can be replicated in so many cities.

The building of a city is a story of strong personalities and human interests, not just one of politics and planning permission, battles and barricades. It is also one of (and I choose my example deliberately) *pleasure*. For any Londoner along the Thames, for any Dubliner or visitor who has ambled along the Liffey, catching a stranger's eye, smiling at a passing scene . . . it is that quality of social life that makes cities live.

And it is that quality—the sheer pleasure of populousness—that we who are in charge of representing urban culture must convey with all its drama in the work we do. In the Museum of London's new redevelopment, the Capital City galleries, the Vauxhall Pleasure Gardens (a great eighteenth-century center of city pleasure and delight, the place where you went to see and be seen) are brought to life by an immersive sound and light experience.

BUILDING A MUSEUM

This chapter has started with high ambitions and no little abstraction: the power of the city, its living presence, the way in which history continues as part of any present urban landscape. That's all very well as a set of ideals, you might object. But how does one attain such qualities in a museum?

Let's begin with the building. Most national museums and galleries "start as buildings—or portions of buildings—in which rulers kept their collections; they developed into buildings which rulers regularly opened to the respectable segment of the public; they finally emerged as buildings belonging to the city or the nation, often on the basis of a royal collection presented to the nation, or commandeered by it."[10] Such an inheritance suited city leaders who wanted grandly designed, central located public buildings (Corinthian columns and all) for show. Subsequent institutions imitated what we now think of as the "museum style," in order to make a claim for their universal (they meant, of course, European) authority.

But the old hierarchies are no longer so clearly defined. The new urban settlement is more fluid and, one would like to think, more responsive to the varieties of cultural difference and change. So any new museum building needs to find a way of creating a new national and civic identity.

Let's take a Chinese example. The new Capital Museum in Beijing is an exciting building, designed by the China Architecture Design and Research Group with the French practice AREP. Its wide modernist eaves are inspired by traditional Chinese architecture; the rotunda bursts like a rocket from the building's glass-roofed facade. It looks very modern. Yet as you enter, you see the enormous red columns and elaborate colors of an imperial gate that dominates the back of the foyer. The contrast is thrilling. What the building does, magnificently, is to represent local tradition within an international aesthetic. It manages to say something old, but to say it in a completely modern way.

The location of such buildings is equally important. A city museum will draw much of its power from just the sort of connections with the city discussed earlier. The Addis Ababa Museum in Ethiopia overlooks the enormous, inescapable immensity of Meskel Square in the city center. It is hard to imagine the museum having anywhere near the same impact tucked away down a set of side streets or lost in the tree-lined enclave of an outer suburb. For here, as you enter the museum or look out from it, is the heart of the city itself, its open space, its sky. The building leads into the life of Addis Ababa, from its traffic roaring past to the aspirations and competing pleasures of its sports stadium.

Such gestures are not merely symbolic. In the hard reality of the cultural economy, city museums need to be closely linked with the civic authority's broader intentions for tourism, leisure, housing, or immigration. Museum leaders have a responsibility to support their city and, of course, can benefit hugely in return.

Making outward contact with the capital—in terms of architecture, situation, attitude—is essential. Looking in, we can define needs that are particular to city museums. At the core of any museum is its collection. The public is at times bemused at what is on display in museums, because they imagine one just sat down one day and chose what one wanted to use to tell the history of the city.

Most people are unaware of that strange process of historic formation that goes into almost any museum collection. The first director of the Museum of London used to ride around on his horse, pointing out bits and pieces of the city he wanted. Things were donated, purchased, acquired. There was nothing so pragmatic as a collections policy. As a consequence, the Museum of London collection contains several fine views of . . . Calcutta.

For historians of culture, such objects reveal the ethos of the time in which they were acquired. But pragmatically, the Museum of London has limited display space and a particular story to tell—which is not the story, fascinating though it would be, of West Bengal.

And yet . . . we need to strike a balance. Yes, the collection needs to decide what does and does not belong to it. The problem of accession and de-accession is fundamental, and one that the public is rarely aware of. It requires careful thought not just of what is needed now, but what may be needed in the future. Today's ephemera are tomorrow's rarity.

But to some extent London, like many major cities from New York to Moscow, is a product of many different cultures and groups. A colonial view of Calcutta may not be of immediate relevance, but a *salwar kameez* worn by women in northern India and Pakistan is. One such outfit is displayed at the Museum not just because it shows the shirt, trousers, and *chuni* (the scarf) that can be seen on the streets of London today, but because it has become part of the capital's culture. The design became fashionable in the 1990s. Celebrities from Princess Diana to Cherie Blair, the wife of the former prime minister, appeared in public wearing the *salwar kameez*, and the women's suit in the Museum was in fact made in London, in Brick Lane in Spitalfields, East London, which has become a center of Bangladeshi culture. If people encounter such a display and walk up to it wondering what on earth it's doing in the Museum of London, or any such museum of a city, then that is pleasing because it means they will discover something new about the capital, something less obvious than they might have expected, something as a tourist, for instance, that they might never see.

An international outlook is therefore essential: City museums must not be parochial. Whether it is outward-looking design such as that of the Capital Museum, Beijing, or displays such as the *salwar kameez*, the aim must be to establish local interest, but within an international outlook. And our explanations, too, must mirror the largest thinking possible. To discuss the Hôtel des Invalides at the edge of Paris (as it then was), built to care for soldiers and invalids, is not just to reveal the lives of Parisians, though that may be the reason we choose to discuss it in the first place. It is equally to establish possible analogies with, among others, say, the Royal Hospital, Chelsea in London, built for similar purpose in the sixteenth and seventeenth centuries. Paris is here, but Paris is also part of a world culture.

AMBITIONS

There are, of course, other issues in museum life today—some might call them pressures, or opportunities. The notion that we can choose a site, construct a building, and place things on display is no longer a straightforward one. It's worth spending a bit of time getting underneath what some of these issues are.

The social function of *public* museums has been at their heart from the very beginning. Museums and galleries have always been places of contest, on the one hand aiming to be "temples of art" for the cognoscenti, and on the other hand looking to educate and improve a mass public.[11] This can be forgotten amid present concerns about widening audiences and improving access and diversity. This debate about whom museums are for has been going on, in differing terms, for a very long time and should not be dismissed as a passing fad. Public collections should be for . . . the public.

There is something dispiriting at times about the rhetoric of access. The (English) Museums, Libraries and Archives Council has produced a set of guidelines called *Access for All*.[12] This "toolkit," as they dub it, is completely well-meaning in its intentions: It really does intend organizations to find ways of scrutinizing what they do to improve their relations with their public. That is admirable, but as it talks of user outcomes, community profiling, structures to enable participation, one's heart sinks. Users are people; outcomes are lives that have been changed. It is as if bureaucratic language has sunk the project before it has even begun.

But it has not, of course. Museums do an enormous amount of good work for the community. As the report *Museums and Social Inclusion* suggests, not only can museums create powerful places of learning that are nonjudgmental and unassociated with "problems" and social failing—one of the most basic qualities a museum can share is its aura of success—but museums can also fundamentally "represent and express a vision of an inclusive society."[13] The ambition is high, and the standard a tough one for museums to continue to meet. Museums do an enormous amount of good to fight social exclusion, but much of the work is, as one analyst argues, unfocused and "fuzzy."[14] It may be that museums need to target more specific audiences rather than aiming for a generalized inclusiveness.

The issue of access is raised in part because cultural institutions, especially those in the city center, are in competition in many respects with consumer culture. Commercial environments increasingly woo purchasers less with products than with their associated lifestyles. Shopping centers are now places of entertainment, whose symbolic design and atmosphere of inclusion for all, as Sharon Zukin persuasively argues, make a bid for ownership over public life.[15] The message is, especially for young people: We are what we shop. If museums are to prosper in such a competitive context, they have to assert their own definition not just of who was here, but of who belongs here now. Widening that definition broadens the basis of their claim to social importance and cultural centrality.

If widening access is as much an act of self-preservation as of social policy, it sits alongside another necessary consideration for any new museum, which is sustainability. The word is another which gets bandied about to the point of meaninglessness. But it has meaning, and an important one. The architect Richard Rogers in his search for a future architecture writes of "the sustainable city."[16] He rightly does not limit this to ecological impact (though he is gravely concerned about managing resources effectively in making new buildings), but understands a complex set of sustaining relationships for the city: its connections to systems of education and health, food and justice; its points of contact and creativity; its beauty and animation; in part as a result of diversity thriving, being renewed, growing.

He places change at the center of what cities are, and he speaks of an "active citizenship" in which citizens are involved in the evolution of their city and feel that public space is in their communal ownership and responsibility.[17] Such a vision is enthralling, because it means that a Museum of London or of Addis Ababa or of Beijing has a key role for the very citizens it hopes to represent. Public collections foster a sense of civic identity—not by delimiting what that identity is, but by handing it over conceptually to the city. The collection is a movable thing, possible of any number of configurations. As long as we, its guardians, keep saying to the city "Who are you?" "What do you do?" "What do you need?" our museums will remain both topical and top-notch.

CAPTURING CHANGE

It is hoped that the dynamism a city museum can generate by establishing and exploring its relationships to the city has been described adequately. Any city is much more than content for such a museum. And what content there is can only suffer by cowering fearfully in the curatorial vault, frightened that it can never make sense of the fast-changing spree that most cities are. It goes against the traditional museum mindset to leap into the current—and that is exactly what we ought to do!

What about capturing change in city museums? Earlier we discussed two sorts of internationalism. One sort of museum model provides local interest and attention (as in Beijing) but remains international in outlook. Looking at museum ambitions for our time, we can see that audiences too (residents and visitors) are comprised of a diverse mix of cultures that provide their own international content for any city museum.

Where these two internationalisms meet is, in fact, at the very nexus of multicultural change that museums need to celebrate. In a rather witty essay entitled "Mess Is More," architects Robert Venturi and Denise Scott Brown celebrate twenty-first-century urban chaos. They single out Tokyo as

> *the* city most relevant and revealing for our time. It's no longer Paris for its formal/spatial and symbolic unity, or New York for its technical grandeur. . . . It is Tokyo exemplified by integrated chaos involving sublime relationships engaging complexities and contradictions, and juxtapositions and ambiguities of scale, space, form and especially cultural symbolisms.
>
> There is no question concerning Japan's original genius for a cultural system, deep and broad within its dimensions, but also exclusive, and its current genius for acknowledging what we call multiculturalism—for adopting and adapting foreign influences and for juxtaposing them in creative ways that create chaos valid for today.[18]

Here, then, is a city of our time: It blends both old culture and new; it is not a mosaic of carefully placed cultural pieces but a busy, captivating, self-contradicting blur of neon lights and cultural contradictions. Are Venturi and Scott Brown troubled by this? Of course not. They're postmodernists—they're not troubled by anything! But their point about modernity in the city is right: We need to see multiculturalism as a living thing, moving and changing. Cities are fed by the influences of the world, and if a museum (the very word can begin to sound outdated in such a context) is going to feel like the city, it has to establish a dialogue with these ongoing shifts and turns—not mimic them, but know that this is how the city feels to anyone leaping into a taxi or trying to call for a drink at the bar.

Let us not forget, people pass through cities. London's vast Heathrow Airport has more employees than a large English city—but traditionally, it is hard to get Heathrow into the museum narrative. Again, many cities in Britain and elsewhere in western Europe have large numbers of Polish immigrants, following the entry of Poland into the European Union. Dublin, Ireland's capital, has more Poles per capita even than London. It is how the city is right now. But would a museum of Dublin know how to represent that reality?

When you ask outsiders about London, Prague, Rome, Amsterdam, Paris, they immediately refer to the highspots, the clichés. The language of tourism? Perhaps, but no less potent for being so. In the end, all city museums either seize or succumb to an urban brand. Such cultural identities may occur, to quote one social geographer,

> through the forging of a connection between a particular city and a personality (Joyce's Dublin, Gaudí's Barcelona), stressing the key contribution of a major landscape or prestige project (such as the Guggenheim museum in Bilbao) or highlighting a major cultural or sporting event (the Venice Biennale, the Monaco Grand Prix or the Edinburgh Festival).[19]

But here too, capturing change is important. All brands have a sell-by date,[20] and so monitoring what's happening in the city ensures that one is no longer offering the Dublin of James Joyce when it's really the Dublin of Flann O'Brien they're clamoring for. And one isn't saying: "Look. We're a museum in a box. It's all safe and neatly packaged." Cities aren't like that, and no more should a city museum be.

NOTES

1. Richard Stanyhurst, "The Description of Ireland" in Raphael Holinshed, *The Chronicles of England, Scotland and Ireland* (1577; London: Henry Denham, 1587), vol. 2, chap. 3, "The Names of the Civities, Boroughs and Haven Townes in Ireland," 20, col. 1, 11.71–74, col. 2, 11.1–5.

2. Stanyhurst, "Description of Ireland," in Holinshed, vol. 2, chap. 3, 20, col. 1, 11.44–45.

3. Patrick Geddes, *Cities in Evolution* (1914), cited in paraphrase from Spiro Kostof, *The City Shaped: Urban Patterns and Meanings through History* (London: Thames & Hudson, 1991), 86.

4. Geddes, *Cities in Evolution*, cited in Kostof, *City Shaped*, 86.

5. James Malton, *Picturesque and Descriptive View of the City of Dublin* (1799), cited in Mark Girouard, *Cities and People: A Social and Architectural History* (New Haven, CT: Yale University Press, 1985), 219.

6. Stanyhurst, "Description of Ireland," in Holinshed, vol. 2, ch. 3, 20, col. 2, 11.5–11.

7. Charles Dickens, *Bleak House* (1853), chap. 1, 1.

8. Quoted in Girouard, *Cities and People*, 188.

9. Girouard, *Cities and People*, 189.

10. Girouard, *Cities and People*, 330. See also Tony Bennett, *The Birth of the Museum: History, Theory, Politics* (London: Routledge, 1995), 17–58.

11. Bennett, *Birth of the Museum*, 89–91. See also Eileen Hooper-Greenhill, "The Museum in the Disciplinary Society," in *Museum Studies in Material Culture*, ed. J. Pearce (Leicester: Leicester University Press, 1989).

12. *"Access for All" Toolkit: Enabling Inclusion for Museums, Libraries and Archives*, (London: Museums, Libraries and Archives Council, 2004).

13. *Museums and Social Inclusion*, GLLAM Report (Group for Large Local Authority Museums): Research undertaken by the Research Center for Museums and Galleries (RCMG), Department of Museum Studies, University of Leicester, October 2000, 49. Museums are unusual in being able to share their attributes of success and authority with the socially excluded, in part because they lack the taint of "problem" contexts that prisons, social services, and so forth are associated with through their work with the marginalized.

14. Graham Black, *The Engaging Museum: Developing Museums for Visitor Involvement* (London: Routledge, 2005), 51.

15. Sharon Zukin, "Space and Symbol in an Age of Decline," in *Re-Presenting the City: Ethnicity, Capital and Culture in the Twenty-First-Century Metropolis*, ed. Anthony D. King (London: Macmillan, 1996), 55. See also Sharon Zukin, *The*

Culture of Cities (Oxford: Blackwell, 1995). Glenn Lowry, director of MOMA, warns of the opposite movement: that cultural competition may in fact be a blurring in both directions. How different are museums themselves from shop displays of jewelry you can buy? See Glenn Lowry, "A Deontological Approach to Art Museums and the Public Trust," in *Whose Muse? Art Museums and the Public Trust*, ed. James Cuno (Princeton, NJ: Princeton University Press, 2004), 129–149.

16. Richard Rogers and Philip Gumuchdjian, *Cities for a Small Planet* (London: Faber & Faber, 1997), 169.

17. Rogers and Gumuchdjian, *Cities for a Small Planet*, 16.

18. Robert Venturi and Denise Scott Brown, "Mess Is More," in *Urban Visions: Experiencing and Envisioning the City*, Tate Liverpool Critical Forum, vol. 5, ed. Steven Spier (Liverpool: Liverpool University Press, 2002), 153.

19. Phil Hubbard, *City* (London: Routledge, 2006), 86–87.

20. Hubbard, *City*, 87.

6

Thinking the Present Historically at the Museum of Sydney

CAROLINE BUTLER-BOWDON AND SUSAN HUNT

In less than a generation, metropolitan Sydney has been transformed in almost every conceivable way. Its economic base has shifted to new growth sectors; its population has swollen and become vastly more diverse; and housing choices, for those who can afford them, have expanded. And as Sydney edges up the hierarchy of global cities, questions of environmental sustainability, social justice, governance, urban design, and the overall quality of life engage daily conversation, attract increasing media coverage, and demand appropriate public policy responses.[1]

How does a city museum respond to the multiple histories of its place and the complexity of a contemporary city as diverse as Sydney? The exercise is both possible and impossible. Possible through clever programming of the ordinary and extraordinary, providing partial responses to the history of the city. Impossible because a city museum cannot offer comprehensiveness. Indeed, the Museum of Sydney *on the site of first Government House* has long debated what the title of a city museum really means and whether, given its small physical size, it can be a city museum or rather an interesting museum in the city.

A common imperative shared by urban history museums is relevance to their contemporary city and its people as well as to visitors from afar. Sydney is one of the most recognizable cities in the world, the subject of considerable international and national focus in the past ten years. For those overseas, Sydney often represents a cardboard cutout of utopian life: harbor, beaches, lush gardens, sunny climate, and carefree people. This image is relayed via tourism campaigns, soap operas, and other sorts of distorted cultural products. For those who live in Australia and indeed in Sydney, the reality, of course, is somewhat different. As the Museum of Sydney (MOS), there is an expectation to encapsulate the broader history: to meet international expectations with a focus on landmark places and events, without losing sight of the need to remain relevant to the city's own citizens.

This chapter outlines some of the ways in which MOS contributes to discussion in the city by reaching a broad audience of constituents across a range of cultural programs. Other institutions, including the city's cultural partners and competitors, museums, societies, architectural and urban associations, and community groups, also provide debates, discussions, and exhibitions on contemporary issues. MOS needs to differentiate itself in a crowded "talks" and cultural market. Fortunately, museums are uniquely placed to position contemporary debates about city issues within a historical frame: to "think the present historically."[2]

> We travel backward in time through memory and through the recorded imagery of paintings, photographs, the cinema, and architecture. . . . These collections bracket history from their own point of view, recomposing the artifact's context through a network of references and comparative rereading that resituate the past in the present. . . . These are the ways in which we frame the city, visually imagining its form and materially reconstituting its structure: by travel, in the theatre, at the museum, from the cinema.[3]

In this way the past assists us in making sense of the contemporary city. Historic artifacts in the context of contemporary urban life provide museums with a unique way to become places for the discussion of contemporary issues.

HISTORY OF MOS

Opened in 1995, MOS is a modern museum on a historic site. The museum is built on the site of the earliest foundations of British colonialism in Australia, a place with many layers and meanings. It was on this site that Governor Arthur Phillip built the first Government House in 1788—the home, office, and seat of authority for the first nine British governors of New South Wales until it was demolished in 1846. Conversely, the site was also the point of first contact between the Cadigal people of Sydney and the British exiles arriving on the First Fleet. It is therefore a symbol of invasion for Australia's indigenous population.

During the 1980s archaeologists exposed the remains of the house, uncovering thousands of artifacts—fragments of pottery, glass, bone, metal, and building materials excavated from the layers of soil, drains, and foundations. The dig was undertaken following an application to commercially develop the site, given its location in the heart of Sydney's central business district. "The site was vindicated as being of resounding symbolic value to all Australians,"[4] and in 1995 the state-funded MOS opened to interpret this symbolic place and the ongoing story of Sydney.

The museum attracts visitation in the vicinity of 75,000 to 95,000 people (depending on the strength of programming in any given year), with hundreds of thousands more visiting the site and public programs throughout the year. Visitors are 60 percent Australians, with the vast majority of these coming from Sydney and the state of New South Wales in which Sydney is located.[5] The bulk of the audience is tertiary-educated and employed, with marginally more women than men. Given the large numbers of locals who visit MOS, the museum has a necessarily broad focus to interpret the history of Sydney, covering historical and contemporary themes of the city's social, cultural, architectural, and urban history. It is undeniably a broad brief for a small museum to cover.

The pressure to cover a sweep of history culturally and geographically, while remaining relevant to contemporary society, is simultaneously both challenging and liberating in its scope. There is an expressed desire in the programming to encapsulate rich and poor peoples and places, places of monumentality, great events and ordinary lives.

While exhibitions are the museum's core business to drive visitation, both repeat and new visitors, and to raise its profile, the strategy has been to develop a series of high-profile public programs that sometimes relate to the exhibitions but sometimes stand alone. Often the types of material, particularly controversial topics, lend themselves more easily to discussions at the museum rather than to the necessarily slow-moving arena of exhibition-making.

AUSTRALIA'S LARGEST "ETHNICITY"

Sydney has become a metropolis of considerable cultural diversity, evidenced by the 249 birthplaces recorded in the 2001 census. Out of 4.1 million Sydney residents, 1.4 million were born overseas. At 32 percent, the overseas-born proportion of Sydney's population is consistent with those of several global cities. If second-generation migrants are included, the overseas-born and their Australian-born children comprise 52 percent of the metropolitan population. In comparison,

> The overseas-born proportion in Toronto, Canada, is 45%, a metropolis commonly ranked with San Francisco, Brussels, Moscow, Seoul, Madrid, Zurich and Sydney itself. London has 27% overseas, while Los Angeles and New York have over 30%.[6]

To capture the living cultures of the city's dwellers, MOS has produced a number of exhibitions, community days, site tours, and talks with different communities, including those originating from India, Vietnam, the South Pacific, China, Italy, and Greece.

One of the most successful programs was a public program developed over a number of years titled the Reclaiming the Past and Changing Sydney series.[7] It provided an opportunity to experience important cultural, spiritual, and commercial sites and to meet members of Sydney's diverse communities. A series of seminars at the museum and bus tours to specific areas of Sydney invited visitors to explore the cultural traditions of many of Sydney's 249 birthplaces. These included exploring the language, painting, and calligraphy of Chinese Australians on Sydney's North Shore; visiting thriving businesses with Southeast Asian connections and feasting on authentic food; a visit to Wat Khemarangsaram, the Khmer Buddhist Temple in Bonnyrigg in Sydney's western suburbs, as people prepared to make offerings to dead loved ones and to seek peace with Buddha; a visit to the Polish Club in the city's inner west to see performances by Syrenka dancers; a program with Muslim communities, spending time at mosques and discussing issues and challenges with Muslim Australian women; and visiting the Uruguayan Club in outer western Sydney to see tango and folklore dancers.

My City of Sydney

One of the recent initiatives aimed at expressing the city's diverse cultures was an exhibition titled My City of Sydney, curated by Susan Hunt, which focused on an eighteen-minute film produced by MOS in which a range of Sydneysiders tell personal stories of places significant to them. The film, together with a broader exhibition about Sydney places and people, did not attempt to characterize Sydney definitively, but to convey a contemporary city of many paradoxes, contradictions, and diverse histories. The stories looped from past to present, conjuring up the city through vignettes of these six sites. The sites range from the dramatic and iconic Sydney Opera House on Bennelong Point to a western suburbs mosque to the Royal National Park to a former hospital site, now a correctional facility.

Welcome to Sydney

The photographic exhibition Welcome to Sydney[8] portrayed the city's multicultural diversity, including nationalities with a long history of migration to Australia, such as Chinese and Italians, and more recent arrivals including Vietnamese, South Africans, and Afghans. Leading Sydney photographer Anne Zahalka invited her subjects to include an object that represents a personal or cultural association with their homeland. By contrast, the locations chosen for the images reflect their new life in Sydney. The project was an important social document in the recent climate of intense controversy over Australia's immigration policies and treatment of refugees. The photographs invited the viewer to question stereotypes of national identity.

Although Bondi Beach is usually depicted on postcards with suntanned lifeguards, Zahalka's portrait of Rabbi Mendel Kastel and his family reminds us that the area is also home to a large Jewish community. Other portraits reference the intricate layers of Sydney's mixed population. Chinese gardener Guangan Wu is pictured in market gardens adjoining the runways of Sydney Airport. Like Sydney itself, the gardens have been successively cultivated over two centuries by different ethnic groups: Irish, Cornish, German, and Chinese.[9] The project was originally commissioned by the Sydney Airports Corporation, which installed a number of the photographs on lightboxes in the group arrivals area of the international terminal. The full set was displayed at MOS and became part of the permanent collection on completion of the exhibition.

Encouraging communities to "own" exhibitions and events takes time. We have consistently found that the most satisfying and meaningful events are those that function as a shared partnership. This type of programming and community consultation is, as all museum workers concede, very time-intensive, but absolutely critical. There is a consistent imperative to continue working with the communities with established bonds while also working up new projects with new communities to diversify the audience and build the audience to reflect the highly diverse Sydney metropolitan population.

INDIGENOUS HISTORY AND COLONIAL HISTORY

Perhaps the museum's most important work has been the development of permanent and temporary programs that focus on the city's indigenous and colonial histories—investigations of the city's turbulent colonial history from a contemporary perspective. To continue to live in a postcolonial country such as Australia and work on such a significant site demands a sustained engagement with the city's indigenous people, the Cadigal people of the Eora nation who lived here before white occupation in 1788.

The Sydney descendants of the Cadigal form part of the largest single concentration of indigenous people in Australia. While the traditionally strong concentration of indigenous people in inner-city suburb Redfern still exists, there are larger numbers in the outer suburbs. One of MOS's most satisfying collaborations was a 1997 exhibition titled Guwanyi: Stories of the Redfern Aboriginal Community. For this project, MOS curatorial and exhibition staff worked with an indigenous curator and artists including Brenda Croft, Michael Riley, and Elaine Kitchener to produce a photographic exhibition of the streets and life of Redfern. It told the experiences of the inner-city indigenous population through photographs and text. One of the collaborators summed it up:

> I've now been living in and around the "Fern" for most of my life. I still call Moree home but my heart's in Redfern. I've been lucky to be part of this community. It's given me a strength that I don't believe I would have got from anywhere else. My work has always been here, although I did what most young Kooris do, and that is have a go out in the big, white world, but Redfern draws you back.[10]

Staff at MOS are acutely aware that more can and should be done with indigenous communities in terms of education, exhibition, and public programming. There have been real successes in this area, though. In collaboration with the Sydney Festival 2004, Australia Council for the Arts, and the performing arts company Legs on the Wall, MOS produced a spectacular yet poignant physical theater piece, *Eora Crossing*; it took place on First Government House Place and the exterior of MOS for three continuous nights with huge attendance.

> As smoke rises from freshly burnt eucalypt leaves,
> ancient Australia meets our modern world. . . .
> Graceful, isolated journeys over Australia's outback terrain,
> proud iconic indigenous dancers slowly edging over
> the rooftops towards the ground we stand on

Combining traditional indigenous dance with fast-paced acrobatics, *Eora Crossing* brought together European and indigenous worlds on the site of the colony's first Government House for a mass audience.

On a daily basis, the museum's core education program "Whose place is it anyway?" is very effective in raising issues of indigenous history through a specific Sydney focus for school-age children. It is an interactive program that develops students' understanding and appreciation of the culture of the original Sydney Aboriginal peoples, the impact of British colonization, and the place of the Cadigal (the indigenous peoples of Sydney) in the city's history. These temporary exhibitions and programs are underpinned by a permanent presence of indigenous history in the museum, some of the most powerful displays at MOS.

As you approach the museum, on the forecourt is the museum's signature piece, a contemporary sculptural installation, *Edge of the Trees*, by two artists, one Aboriginal and one non-Aboriginal. The title and concept reflect the moment when the Cadigal people watched, from the edge of the trees, as the strangers of the First Fleet struggled ashore in 1788. This sculptural installation by Janet Laurence and Fiona Foley symbolizes that first encounter. Richly embedded with materials and language, the sculpture evokes layers of memory, people, and place. As one crosses the threshold of the museum, a soundscape is heard that is a modern poem based on the original diaries of First Fleet astronomer William Dawes, documenting conversations with his Aboriginal companion, Patye. These intimate cross-cultural exchanges, born in the crucible of colonization, still have poignancy.

On the top level of MOS the visitor can find Cadigal Place, a gallery that honors the history, culture, and survival of the Cadigal clan on whose land this museum stands. One permanent display is a powerful video montage, "Eora" (meaning "people" in the language of the Cadigal clan of Sydney), created for MOS at its opening by Michael Riley. It takes the viewer on a filmic journey, accompanying an Aboriginal family from Redfern as they retrace the steps of the Eora, through sites and memories to their dreaming.[11]

In tandem with the exploration of indigenous life, MOS has mounted a series of exhibitions and talks that are part of an ongoing investigation of colonial encounter, which the museum has explored since 1995. Exhibitions dedicated to early European encounters with Terra Australis—its inhabitants, its landscape, and its flora and fauna—have been at the core of the museum's programming. These have included Fleeting Encounters;

Terre Napoleon: Australia through French Eyes 1800–1804; and An Exquisite Eye: The Work of Ferdinand Bauer.

DEBATING AND TALKING ABOUT THE CITY

"Sydney talks about urban issues that matter in various ways: through informal conversation, on talk-back radio, at professional symposiums, lectures and seminars, in parliamentary debates and countless bureaucratic meetings. Many productive exchanges, discoveries and insights are never recorded or circulate only among the cognoscenti, perhaps via limited distribution government publications or specialised academic research reports."[12] The museum seeks to make a publicly accessible record of Sydney debates, bringing together informed stakeholders from across the spectrum of Sydneysiders.

In developing exhibitions and programs, MOS does not work in isolation. The preference is to form partnerships to stage events and exhibitions. For example, a series of three conferences titled Talking about Sydney (2003–2005) was forged with the University of New South Wales's City Futures program. By sharing resources, including intellectual resources, the museum was able to invite better speakers, attract larger audiences, and gain more currency in the contemporary market of city discussion.

As the dean of the Faculty of the Built Environment at the University of New South Wales and the then head of MOS argued,

> Cities are complex reflections of social, political, economic and cultural forces. These forces produce physical outcomes in the built environment, ranging from individual buildings through to neighborhoods, districts and entire metropolitan regions. As conditions change so do physical forms, typically at a time lag but cumulatively over time. [The physical forms] reflect the legacy of historical conditions no longer in play with an overlay of powerful contemporary forces."[13]

These overlays have never been more noticeable in Sydney than today, when you wander the streets and see the massive changes wrought in a postindustrial world and the enormous changes brought by the cultural and ethnic mix of peoples that Sydney attracts.

At MOS, considerable intellectual capital has been invested in the belief that the city is a topic for ongoing debate in our daily lives. Over the past fifteen years, MOS has developed a range of conferences that explore a broad spectrum of ideas on the city from a range of interdisciplinary approaches. In the Debating the City series of conferences ("Debating the City 1: City Living and Cosmopolitanism"; "Debating the City 2: Urban Visions Public Space"; and "Debating the City 3: Consuming Spaces"), aspects of city life were analyzed from varying and often conflicting viewpoints, including those of geographers, architects, cultural commentators, sociologists, writers, and journalists, to tackle the complex anatomy of this all-embracing topic.

In this series, MOS went beyond the academic arena because these voices are often those already heard in the public arena. Instead, for instance, a shopping mall designer was encouraged to analyze the topic of urban renewal and sociability and the changes in the retail industry to meet consumer demands; a fiction writer took the museum on a heady journey beneath the "picture postcard" surface of Sydney to expose a clever juxtaposition of the city's glamorous exterior with its gritty underbelly; an environmental lawyer described his own environmentally sustainable makeover of an inner-city terrace house; and an indigenous curator and artist took us on highly personal journey challenging the way white Australian history acknowledges places of historical significance, with details of urban developments that have forced the displacement of indigenous people. Some of the speakers were locals, some national, and others international.

A major project about Sydney by the founding head curator of MOS, Peter Emmett, included a trilogy of exhibitions—Metropolis, Suburbs, and Harbor and a publication, took the viewer on "an imaginary journey through Sydney, revealing weird and wonderful urban stories about people teasing place out of space." Through art, architecture, design, literature, film, and fantasy, the exhibitions and book reveal "the dreams and deliriums of Sydney people."[14] The Suburbs component went to the heart of Sydney's image:

It's well known that we are amongst the most suburbanized peoples of the world. Most of us were born, grew up and will die in the suburbs. . . . The story of Sydney shows our innate sub-urbanity. This is a history set in streets, rooms and shorelines, not on battlefields or in burnt palaces. It is a story of individual, almost domestic lives, not the sweeping events of revolt and revolution."[15]

HISTORY OF THE CITY AND SUBURBS

While MOS, given its site and its broader umbrella institution, the Historic Houses Trust of New South Wales (HHT), is often identified with the nineteenth rather than the twentieth century, MOS's twentieth- and twenty-first-century focus has expanded during the past twelve years. While MOS uses the past to interpret Sydney's history, its most popular exhibitions usually focus on aspects of twentieth-century history. For example, the exhibition Art Deco explored the impact of this international style on the architecture and design of Sydney. The exhibition's success resulted in part from its positioning of this historical style within the contemporary Sydney of economic and building booms, as well as the "old" Sydney of archival photos and film.

While the HHT is not an advocacy organization, it is understood that "museums do have some very significant advantages in discussions about current issues." As an American museologist said: "Museums are safe places where the community can discuss unsafe ideas."[16] While not directly affecting planning regulations and heritage in the city, MOS and HHT lead by example. Conferences such as "Fibro House: Opera House, Conserving Mid-Twentieth-Century Heritage," jointly undertaken with the New South Wales Heritage Office and Documentation and Conservation of Buildings, Sites and Neighborhoods of the Modern Movement (DOCOMOMO), contribute to debate about heritage issues in a booming city economy.

Other projects such as Sydney Open—first staged in 1996 and continuing every two years—raise the issue of conserving heritage and the successful reuse of heritage buildings for contemporary ends. In this program, loosely modeled on similar events in London, Edinburgh, Paris, Chicago, and elsewhere, hidden architectural treasures are unveiled and opened to the public for the first time. The choice of the buildings includes some of the most carefully conserved heritage buildings. The skillful adaptive reuse of heritage buildings is central to the project—the integration of modern design principles into the old, achieving a transitional form of architecture.

MOS continues to facilitate research about its archaeology. A major recent project, Exploring the Archaeology of the Modern City, involved working with industry partners, La Trobe University, the Sydney Harbor Foreshore Authority, Godden Mackay Logan, the New South Wales Heritage Office, Heritage Victoria, and the City of Sydney. It aimed to rewrite the social history of Sydney by drawing together archaeological and historical information about five key excavation sites in Sydney.

While the museum is more than happy to do populist exhibitions that more often than not are focused on famous places or sites in Sydney such as Bondi or the Sydney Harbor Bridge (exhibitions that have brought in huge numbers), it is also keen to challenge history making by asking questions and dispelling myths through its programming.

HOMES IN THE SKY

The most recent research project has been *Homes in the Sky: A History of Apartment Living in Australia.* Both a book and an exhibition, the project told an alternative urban history of Sydney and Australia's domestic life. Despite the suburban image of Sydney and Australia, a third of Sydneysiders actually live the more urban experience of apartment buildings. With Australian cities currently being remade by an unprecedented apartment boom (with more apartments than houses being built in Sydney, Melbourne, and Brisbane), the museum felt driven to explore the history of this contemporary phenomenon.

The research project built on earlier work by MOS that had given voice to public housing tenants. Tenant by Tenant was a photographic exhibition of work taken by tenants of one of Australia's largest public housing estates, the Northcott estate. The exhibition was part of a project developed by Big hART to develop creative interventions to help rebuild individual and community confidence on the housing estate. Working closely with pho-

FIGURE 6.1
Homes in the Sky exhibition. Apartment living in Sydney. Photo by Jenni
Carter. © Historic Houses Trust of NSW.

tographer Keith Saunders, many of Northcott's one thousand tenants composed portraits of their neighbors, notable for humor, humanity, and grace.[17]

Apartments have been consistently popular with Sydneysiders since their introduction in 1900, forming a significant minority of the city's housing by the 1950s. Histories of housing ignored this alternative domestic history because it did not fit easily with Australia's self-image. Robin Boyd, Australia's leading architectural historian, wrote in 1952 that "Australia is the small house. . . . The suburban way of life and the aspiration to own and occupy a detached house have long been Australian characteristics."[18]

Since Boyd wrote these words in 1952, the association between the suburban cottage and Australian history has become even more of a nationalist touchstone. Despite its popularity, apartment living remains excluded from the patriotic embrace. As symbols of urban cosmopolitanism, apartments were seen as alien imports. Indeed, whenever there is criticism of current apartment developments, they are invariably described in terms of what they represent about globalism: The fact that parts of Sydney now resemble Hong Kong or other Asian cities sparks the inference that the city is losing its identity.

These international influences and connections have been a consistent theme of MOS exhibitions. International collections can contribute new perspectives on Sydney's history. A notable example was Kiichiro Ishida and the Sydney Camera Circle 1920s–1940s. This exhibition from the Shoto Museum of Art, Tokyo, explored "the exchange of art and trade between Japan and Australia, along with the largely unknown story of a thriving and prosperous Japanese community living in Sydney from the 1880s until 1941."[19] The centerpiece of the exhibition was the work of Kiichiro Ishida and other Japanese émigré photographers, prominent interpreters of Sydney during the 1920s and 1930s.

CONCLUSION

MOS has "always been more than a staid custodian of past treasures," preferring to pursue "an expansive communications program intersecting with the culture of the contemporary city in many ways."[20] In showcasing some of the work that has been done at MOS, there is an inbuilt argument for the validity and uniqueness of city museums to remain vital to contemporary audiences. The city of Sydney, for all its contemporary problems and challenges, is a thrilling city full of energy, diversity, and ideas. MOS is here to channel some of this energy, diversity, and ideas by bringing people together to experience aspects of the city's past, present, and future.

NOTES

1. R. Freestone, B. Randolph, and C. Butler-Bowdon, eds., *Talking about Sydney: Population, Community and Culture in Contemporary Sydney* (Sydney: University of New South Wales Press in association with Historic Houses Trust of New South Wales, 2006).

2. F. Jameson, *Postmodernism, or The Cultural Logic of Late Capitalism* (London: Verso, 1991), ix.

3. M. Christine Boyer, *The City of Collective Memory: Its Historical Imagery and Architectural Entertainments* (Cambridge, MA: MIT Press, 1994), 69–70.

4. "Museum of Sydney on the Site of First Government House," *Insites*, Summer 1993.

5. Historic Houses Trust of New South Wales, *Annual Report 2005–2006*, 48–49.

6. G. Hugo, in *Talking about Sydney*, ed. Freestone et al., 42.

7. These two series were developed by Diana Giese, a consultant who worked with MOS to develop the content.

8. The project was curated by John Murphy, who worked with photographer Anne Zahalka. It was shown at the Museum of Sydney, and seventeen of the works were acquired by MOS for the permanent collection.

9. I. Walden, "Exhibition Text Panel and 'Welcome to Sydney,'" *Insites*, Spring 2003, 6–7.

10. C. Craigie, "Redfern," *Guwanyi: Stories of the Redfern Aboriginal Community*, Museum of Sydney exhibition catalog, 21 December 1996–4 May 1997 (Sydney: Museum of Sydney, 1996).

11. I. Walden, "Michael Riley: Artist, Photographer, Filmmaker," *Insites*, Spring 2005, 6–7.

12. Freestone et al., *Talking about Sydney*, ix.

13. P. Murphy and S. Hunt, "Foreword," in *Talking about Sydney*, ed. Freestone et al., vi.

14. P. Emmett, "Sydney Metropolis + Sub-urb + Harbour," *Insites*, Summer 1999, 10–11. The exhibitions were staged at MOS from 18 December 1999 to 3 December 2000.

15. P. Tonkin, "Meditations on the Suburb," *Insites*, Autumn 2000, 6–7.

16. P. Watts, "Foreword," in *Fibro House: Opera House, Conserving Mid-Twentieth-Century Heritage*, ed. Sheri Burke, proceedings of a conference convened by the Historic Houses Trust of New South Wales, 23–24 July 1999 (Sydney: Historic Houses Trust of New South Wales, 2000), xiv.

17. Curated by Inara Walden, Tenant by Tenant opened at MOS in January 2006 as part of the annual Sydney Festival.

18. R. Boyd, *Australia's Home*, 2nd ed. (1952; Melbourne: Penguin, 1978), viii.

19. B. Hise, P. Oliver, and Y. Mitsuda, "Kiichiro Ishida," *Insites*, Summer 2003, 4–5.

20. Freestone et al., *Talking about Sydney*, x.

7

A City Museum for Stuttgart

Some Issues in Planning a Museum for the Twenty-First Century

ANJA DAUSCHEK

Even though it is the sixth-largest city in Germany with a population of nearly six hundred thousand, Stuttgart has never had a museum about itself. Finally, in 2006, the City Council decided to make good this omission and create the Stuttgart City Museum. Planning started in early 2007.

There are three immediate questions: Why a city museum now? What are the conditions for planning the museum? What are the issues the project faces in planning a city museum that is to serve a twenty-first-century audience?

THE STARTING POINTS

The starting point for any museum is either a mission or a collection. In the case of Stuttgart, it was not until the 1930s that anyone started to collect material on the city systematically, and even now there are only about three thousand objects available. Therefore, there is no collection sufficiently comprehensive to predetermine the concept of the museum. So the mission, objectives, and themes of the future museum can and must be developed without the backbone of a strong collection. Yet there is one object that will influence the museum profoundly—the future building.

The city museum will be housed in the centrally located Wilhelmspalais; it was built in the 1830s as the home of the two princesses of Württemberg, Marie and Sophie, and until 1918 it was home to Wilhelm II, the last king of Württemberg. After being used as office and exhibition space, in 1937 it was turned by the Nazi regime into the "Place of Honor of the Achievements of Germans Living Abroad," Stuttgart being the "City of Germans Living Abroad." The building was destroyed in 1944, and its outer walls stood as a ruin until 1961 when it was decided to rebuild it as a library. It has served as the city library since 1965, but the library is now running out of space. So the future museum building is itself an historic object.

FIGURE 7.1
The Wilhelmspalais, the home for the museum. © Klaus Enslin Stuttgart.

FIGURE 7.2
Stuttgart cityscape. © Stuttgart-Marketing GmbH.

However, apart from the building, the lack of a significant collection is not a setback. City museums today are less exclusively focused on a city's history and have evolved into institutions where the city's past, present, and future are discussed. Therefore, being able to develop a city museum based on topics that are relevant to today's citizens is a distinct advantage.

What are the starting points in developing the mission and the themes of the museum? While Stuttgart is as complex a city as any, a few distinctive features stand out:

- Stuttgart and its metropolitan region, with 4.1 million people living within a 50 km range (including a number of separate medium-size cities), is one of the strongest economic regions in Europe. The economy is dominated by tool and car production industries, with well-known global players such as Daimler, Bosch, and Porsche. It is the city where Gottlieb Daimler invented the automobile and Robert Bosch perfected the spark plug, and the region is still known for its innovation potential. In fact, today Stuttgart is the German city with the largest number of listed patents.

- To a substantial extent Stuttgart is an international city. Of its inhabitants, 38.8 percent have a migrant background,[1] the highest percentage of all German cities. Stuttgarters from 170 nationalities live in the city, and together they speak 120 languages.
- Surveys have shown that Stuttgarters consider the city to provide a high quality of life. Satisfaction and confidence characterize the general mood.
- The city topography is rather unusual as the city is neither on a river nor along a major trading route. Downtown is nestled in a bowl surrounded by hills, with the suburbs spread across the hills and the adjacent valleys. The city can best be described as having both a rural and urban character—uniting urban and industrial areas with villages that are still rural.
- The city's history started humbly as a stud farm in the tenth century. Yet soon this small settlement became the residence of the Dukes of Württemberg who became Kings of Württemberg in 1806, following the Napoleonic Wars. As a royal residence it was rather small and exceptional neither in trade nor crafts. Wine making was the major agricultural occupation, as the hilly landscape did not serve other forms of agriculture well. Therefore Stuttgart was a rather small city up to the mid-nineteenth century; the surrounding region was very poor and known only for its high rate of emigration. Industrialization took hold rather late in the 1870s, but subsequently changed the city dramatically in size and character. Despite heavy destruction in the Second World War, the city continued to grow. The war destroyed most of the medieval downtown and literally set the ground for reinventing Stuttgart in the 1950s as a car-friendly city. The city was transformed, and most of the historic structures that had survived the war were pulled down in a program of modernization. The downtown area will again change dramatically over the next decade, as the main train station and rail tracks will be moved underground; one hundred hectares of space will be developed as office and living space, as well as inner-city parks.[2] Given the rather small size of the city center this will again change the city noticeably.

While looking optimistically into the future, the city is facing the basic question of how to maintain a strong economy and at the same time maintain a high quality of life. In doing so, it is aiming to answer these specific questions: How can the increasing percentage of people with migrant backgrounds be successfully integrated with society? How can the city create living conditions that make it attractive for young families to move in and raise children? How can the city create a welcoming atmosphere for those arriving from foreign countries, whether it is for medium- or short-term business or to start a new life?

What can and should the city museum—which is to be opened in 2012—provide for Stuttgart, given that answers to these questions are some of the most fundamental challenges the city faces?

BASIC QUESTIONS FOR A CITY MUSEUM

In 2006, Wolfgang Schuster, the city mayor, stated at the very beginning of the planning process that "the city museum's task is to provide intellectual and emotional orientation based on the city's history, and to offer its visitors, especially children and adolescents, the opportunity to identify with the city and to increase their self esteem as citizens." Accordingly, the planning principles set out in early 2007 aim to ensure that the museum will

- focus on people and their experiences
- connect history to the present and future of the city
- place education at its center
- be visitor-oriented and present an emotional and intellectual experience
- be developed with the active involvement of future stakeholders and visitors

Beyond these basic principles, a number of fundamental questions remain—questions that most probably need to be resolved in planning not only Stuttgart's museum, but in planning city museums in general. They revolve around four factors that define our increasingly globalized world: migration, the individual in society, the feeling of *Heimat*,[3] and the city as a clearly defined place. Each of these factors makes cultural identity and history in cities a contested area and entails yet more questions. For example:

- How important is city history for the cultural identity of its inhabitants, when migration is a defining factor and the complete replacement of a city's existing population may take just ten to twenty years? Is the history of a place still important for the collective and communicative memory of people living in a city whose own roots lie in different cities, other countries, and separate cultures?[4]

- How can the migration experience that is important for a large number of city people be integrated into the museum to become a long-term and sustainable topic? Should a city museum create a *lieu de memoire*—a place for memories—for migrants? But whose memories are to be presented, and by whom? Should nonmigrants learn more about the migration history—or should migrants learn more about the history of the place they have moved to? Here it is important to note that so far Germans and immigrants to Germany have divided memories—a shared memory is still missing. Some writers speak of a "double memory blackout," since Germans do not know the migration history of their own country, nor are migrants familiar with German history. The only migration histories written so far are individual stories relating to work and place of work.[5]

- Individual lifestyles are an important part of city life. Individualism implies the opportunity to define one's own identity, as the sociologist Anthony Giddens points out.[6] Members of many social environments, especially in cities, no longer tie their identity to a place, but rather create it in relation to a specific and often globalized subculture, such as a political movement or music and fashion style. How far history— whether national, regional, or local—is part of this identity-forming process is up to each and every individual.

- The question of place does not make matters easier. City limits have undergone historical change, and they are socially permeable. While cities can be defined by their political and geographical limits, the city as a living space does not keep to these defined borders. Cities influence the region economically and socially, whether, for example, through unstable banlieues like those of Paris and most major world cities, or through the so-called bacon belts, the affluent suburbs of Stuttgart, Munich, and cities virtually everywhere. So what is the geographical range a city museum should adhere to?

- Somewhere between identity and place, there is home—*Heimat*, a feeling, an emotion, a sense of belonging to somewhere or to something that could be quite amorphous and may have no connection to a specific place. As Cicero put it: *Ubi bene, ibi patria*. *Heimat* gained significance in the twentieth century with worldwide migration, and it will gain even greater significance in the twenty-first century—whether the migrant is a well-paid global worker or an economic or political refugee. Should a city museum have a function in creating a feeling of home?

FIRST PLANNING STEPS

These questions are yet to be resolved for the Stuttgart City Museum, but they draw attention to the importance of developing a city museum in discussion with the future audience as well as with specialists from other (city) museums. While focus groups of potential future audiences are being organized as this chapter is written, the project has made an important step forward by bringing together an international group of specialists to discuss the goals and specific objectives of city museums today.[7] This expert group included museum specialists with experience of city, history, and children's museums, as well as specialists in urban and social planning. The specialists' statements as well as the wider discussions in the city have stressed that the museum should be a flexible institution with a vision of the future in order to create an added social value for citizens that could strengthen integration, social cohesion, education, city identity, and community engagement. The museum would be concerned both with the reality of city life and with a vision of the city's future; thus the interplay of creation/action and reflection/observation could be a working model for the museum.

It was considered essential that the museum be relevant to its pluralist constituency and develop questions about interpreting the past that would connect to the present and the future. Therefore, a three-semester research project has been commissioned from the Tübingen University Department of European Ethnography. The following are the questions that need to be answered in order to find the interpretative keys to the city's history: What is relevant to Stuttgarters living in the city today? What moves people in this city; what appeals to them? Why do they see the city as their home—or why don't they? Is there something like a "we" and is it based on, say, shared values or beliefs? At the same time, of course, this project enables the museum to collect the material heritage that represents the communicative memory of Stuttgart.

In the new global economic structure, it has become important for cities to present themselves as unique places in order to foster the creative and the innovative environments that make cities attractive and economically strong. A strong cultural identity is considered one main factor in achieving this.[8] City museums today must go beyond exhibitions about a city's history—they are a city's memory—to be places where the present and the future of a city are put up for debate. City museums should consider it their task to develop questions that critically accompany the development and the design of a city. In so doing, they can navigate a path between their social and cultural remit.[9]

NOTES

1. Having a "migration background" is defined by (1) non-German nationality; (2) place of birth outside Germany; (3) for children below 18 years, having parents who are non-German.

2. See www.stuttgart21.de.

3. *Heimat* describes the feeling of being at home; the emotional connotations of the term are hardly translatable.

4. Maurice Halbwachs coined the term "collective memory" to describe the individual memory set within the context of a social group. See Maurice Halbwachs, *Das kollektive Gedächtnis* (Frankfurt: Fisher, 1985). The term communicative memory (*kommunikatives Gedächtnis*) is defined by Jan Assmann to describe the individual memory transmitted orally, reaching back around eighty to one hundred years. See Jan Assmann, *Das kulturelle Gedächtnis* (Munich: C. H. Beck, 1992).

5. Jan Motte and Rainer Ohlinger, *Geschichte und Gedächtnis in der Einwanderungsgesellschaft* (Essen: Klartext, 2004), 13.

6. Anthony Giddens, *Modernity and Self-Identity: Self and Society in the Late Modern Age* (Cambridge: Polity Press, 2001).

7. The documentation from the Expert Hearing will be published in January 2008. Acknowledgments to David Fleming, Patrick Gallagher, Fabrizio Gallanti, Claudia Haas, Rainer Kazig, Renée Kistemaker, Detlef Kron, Maren Lauster, Klaus Müller, Gari Pavkovic, and Bernhard Tschofen for the discussion.

8. Saskia Sassen, *The Global City: New York, London, Tokyo* (Princeton, NJ: Princeton University Press, 1991); Richard Florida, *The Rise of the Creative Class* (New York: Basic, 2002); Charles Landry, *The Creative City: A Toolkit for Urban Innovators* (London: Earthscan, 2000).

9. Renée Kistemaker, "Epilogue," in *City Museums as Centers of Civic Dialogue: Proceedings of the Fourth Conference of the International Association of City Museums, 3–5 November 2005* (Amsterdam: Amsterdam Historical Museum, 2006), 198.

Taipei City Museum in the Making

CHI-JUNG CHU AND SZU-YUN CHANG

This chapter will outline the Taipei City Museum project to illustrate and examine the functioning of city museums in a non-Western geopolitical context, and the various issues encountered.

Although the Department of Cultural Affairs[1] of the Taipei City Government is the main body in charge, the project involves cross-departmental collaborations and negotiations. By looking at these processes, the chapter will consider how a new museum about a city is reconfiguring the city's cultural and urban landscapes and how the process will shape the museum's policies, its ambitions, and its contribution to the city itself. The intent is to answer three questions: First, has the museum project any features that are different from the contemporary Western experience of city museums? Second, how does a city with a comparatively short history design its city museum, when the classical notion of city museums is so much embedded in history and in authenticating history through material culture? Third, how can the project form an integral but distinctive part of the city's cultural and urban planning agenda, enhance the city's provision of culture, and, further, serve as a hub for both the cultural and social facilities in the neighborhood? To provide the background to the project, we will look into the city's historical trajectory and geographical dimensions.

We will begin by discussing the notion that city museum projects in the West are led primarily by the market rather than by purely cultural considerations.

Culture-led urban regeneration projects have become a popular strategy for postindustrial cities[2] that have experienced industrial decline and high unemployment rates. Museums are often used as key components in cultural regeneration. The successes of the Guggenheim in Bilbao, the Tate Modern in London, the extension to the Louvre in Paris, and similar icons designed by star architects have inspired policy makers and museum practitioners across the world to take on similar projects. However, as the amount of money injected into a cultural regeneration project is usually substantial compared to regular cultural expenditure in the public sector, taking on these projects often involves complicated negotiation processes and usually requires collaboration across different governmental sectors beyond museum and cultural departments themselves. In addition, another problem underlying culture-led regeneration projects is that there is no definitive way to evaluate their effectiveness.[3] Moreover, with the advent of globalization, cities are increasingly replacing nation-states and are becoming geographies of global competition.[4] City museums thus become one of the instruments of local government in city marketing. Just as national museums are the narrative of the state, city museums represent the

Table 8.1

	The historical society and the more traditional city museum	The newer museum of a city
Axis	Time	Space
Time zones	Past	Past, present, and future
Presentations	Two-dimensional form: texts and images	A variety of two- and three-dimensional forms
Contents documentation	Dominated by historical artifacts	Mixture of objects and of the city's past and present, and plans and visions of the city's future

idea of the city, and beyond that, they frequently are used as tools in the wider economic considerations of city governments.

HISTORY AND URBAN DEVELOPMENT OF TAIPEI CITY

The history of Taipei City is closely connected with its economic development, which originated from trade activities along the Tanshui River. The Tanshui River is the city's major river, where indigenous people traded with Westerners and the Chinese not long before the Chinese took over and settled in the eighteenth century. After losing the second Opium War, the failing Ch'ing Court was forced to open Tanshui as an international trading port[5] in 1858, which subsequently brought economic prosperity to Taipei as trade volume increased. Taipei soon replaced Tainan, a city in southern Taiwan that had developed much earlier, and it has been the capital of Taiwan since the island became an independent province of China in 1885.[6] Today, Taipei is a regional or semi-peripheral city in the global economy. It holds a strategic position in the world's economic network, which has been achieved mostly through export-oriented trade activities in the past and more recently by high-tech industries. However, highly polarized domestic political ideologies toward China, together with global competition, have hindered its ambition to become a world city and its other ambition to achieve another economic boom following that of the 1980s.

CITY DEVELOPMENT OF TAIPEI

The urban planning of Taipei City began in the latter half of the nineteenth century, led by the Chinese. Taipei was then one of the first cities in China to encounter westernization and modernization. However, the planning of the city did not last long, as Taiwan was ceded to Japan in 1895 as a result of the first Sino-Japanese War (1894–1895). It is generally acknowledged that Japan's colonial rule (1895–1945) started the process of modernization and set up the infrastructure for Taiwan's subsequent development.

Japan demolished Taipei's city walls in 1904, although the city gates are still in existence today. Under colonial rule, the city center remained in the western section along the Tanshui River but was starting to develop eastward. Though the master urban plan for Taipei did not come to fruition

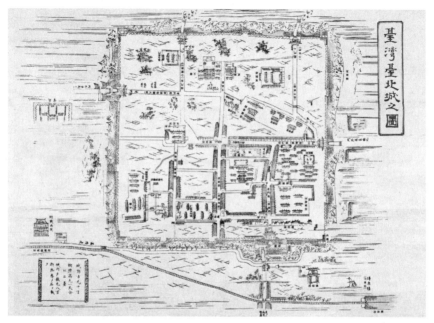

FIGURE 8.1
Taipei city wall. © Department of Cultural Affairs, Taipei City Government.

until 1932,[7] the modern look of Taipei was already taking shape. Straight roads, public buildings of grand Western architectural styles, department stores, coffeehouses, a railway station and railway hotel, a full-fledged museum, a broadcasting station, and public parks were all built within a short period of time, and an international exhibition was held. Taiwan and Taipei were considered as the model for Japan's imperial expansion.

As the capital city of Taiwan, Taipei has been its political, cultural, and financial center since the nineteenth century. The development of the city began in the west end—that is, trade activities in and around the port—and expanded eastward at various stages of the government's urban planning projects. The eastern part of the city has become the downtown, while many of its western parts, which were already in decline, have now become targets of new urban regeneration projects.

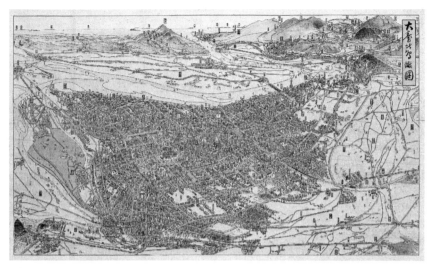

FIGURE 8.2
Taipei in the early twentieth century. © Department of Cultural Affairs, Taipei City Government.

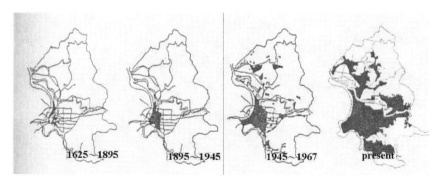

FIGURE 8.3
The growth of Taipei. © Department of Urban Development, Taipei City Government.

FIGURE 8.4
Downtown Taipei today. © Chi-jung Chu.

Meanwhile, high-speed economic expansion and development has been at the expense of the quality of life and the loss of green space, making many parts of the city overcrowded and sometimes ugly. Many of the current tasks of the Department of Urban Development have been concerned with transforming the urban landscape into a greener, more sustainable environment.

THE BIRTH OF THE TAIPEI CITY MUSEUM PROJECT

Taiwanese cultural planning has a habit of emulating successful examples in the West and Japan. As the capital of Taiwan, Taipei is often the first to receive new ideas and practices from the global cultural arena. Several well-known city or historical museums established in the West and in Japan have already provided templates. Moreover, Shanghai and Beijing have both caught up and established new city museums, which have proved popular. As Taipei strives for international exposure, building a city museum has become one of its aims as a global player.

In any event, Taipei has never had a museum dedicated to the city, or indeed a historical society or the equivalent. Although the National History Museum is located in the city, the museum's collections have been more about Chinese rather than Taiwanese history or the history of Taipei. Nevertheless, there has been a quasi–city museum—the Discovery Center of Taipei, run by the city government's Department of Information[8] since its establishment in 2002. The Discovery Center is in an awkward and fragmented location within the city government's main building, and it has not developed as a professionally run museum as was originally planned.

The rapid changes in the city's economic structure resulted in massive changes to the urban landscape. Trade activities along the Tanshui River gradually declined as the river became stagnant. As the urban landscape becomes increasingly disconnected with the past, it is consequently more difficult to find a way to mediate memory, apart from two-dimensional means such as photographs, archives, memorabilia, and documents. Most of these two-dimensional forms are buried in libraries or storage and thus have no immediate visual presence. It is the scant traces of history in the city's landscape that provide an opportunity for building a new museum.

Table 8.2.   Taipei City Museum Project: Fact Sheet

Budget	US$125 million[a]
Design period	3 years
Construction	3 years
Opening year	2012
Total land size	2 hectares
Architectural features	Green architecture
Geographical area	Taipei metropolis[b]

[a] Equivalent to NT$4 billion
[b] Including Taipei City and the satellite cities/counties surrounding the city

The idea of the city museum project was originated by several cultural elites[9] from the nonpublic sector, and it was soon endorsed by the then mayor in 2003. Despite the mayor's support for the project, its progress in the beginning was slow, for a variety of reasons. It was not until the present mayor and the new director of the Department of Cultural Affairs came to office in 2006 that the project was given a boost by a handsome budget increase.

ENVISIONING A NEW CITY MUSEUM

After a lengthy consultation process, the Department of Cultural Affairs decided to locate the museum in the Yuan-shan area. The museum site was once intended to house the Embassy of Saudi Arabia, but it was never built. At present, the site is used as a parking lot and a sports ground. The current progress of the museum project has not reached the stage of finalizing exhibition themes, although the Department of Cultural Affairs has commissioned research institutes to draft ideas for the overall development of the museum. The following ideas and directions are being proposed for future development.

Curatorial

The city museum would provide a legitimate space for making the city the central concern, rather than being subject to the aesthetics of art museums or to political ideology. Two characteristics of the city's history and present condition offer a rich background for contextualizing the new museum's contents. The first lies in the rich diversity of people who have lived in Taipei. In addition to the indigenous people who had lived in the city before the arrival of Chinese settlers in the eighteenth century and the colonial influence from Japan, the Nationalist Government retreated to Taiwan in 1949[10] with about two million soldiers, officials, and civilians from various parts of mainland China. This sudden influx not only created temporary political turmoil but also changed the social and cultural composition of the country—especially in the capital city. In the Cold War period, when the nationalist government was in alliance with the United States, Taiwan, as "Free China," was heavily assisted and influenced by U.S. aid programs in various ways. Being the capital, Taipei has thus shaped a hybrid culture under the influence of a varied political and cultural background. Today, this background is further complicated by migrant workers from Southeast Asia and foreign brides from mainland China, Indonesia, and Vietnam.

The other characteristic lies in the rapid changes that have taken place within the relatively short period of time since 1945. The city used to be the center for agriculture-related trade; it became a center for producer services during the 1960s and 1970s. With the state's centralized economic planning and restructure, the city further changed into an "interface city" as a subcontractor for advanced economies like the United States and Japan.[11] These changes in economic structure resulted in great changes in the urban landscape and in people's lifestyles.

In response to the background sketched above, there are three guiding principles in shaping the museum's contents: changes in urban landscapes, reconstruction of the past, and envisioning the future. There is no definite design or approach, but taken together these principles will weave the texture of the new museum project.

Research

Though research is considered one of the fundamental aspects of museum practice, several universities and research institutes already have research departments that specialize in the study of the city;[12] hence it would be unrealistic to overlap resources and inject money to create another research department within the new museum. However, Taipei City Museum can play a role in integrating these research resources across different disciplinary areas, just as it is expected to help integrate cultural resources across various organizations in the city.

Collections Acquisition

Whether or not to build a collection has been a common problem encountered by new museum projects. In the past, collections usually preceded the creation of the museum itself: Museums were built to house collections. The practices in the contemporary context in which the Taipei City Museum will operate are different, in that so often museums are built to construct ideas. Since the ideas are not necessarily realized through collecting activities, collecting does not constitute an indispensable part of museum activities. This is especially so because, in the contemporary context, to build a substantive, quality collection from scratch has proved to be a difficult financial task for most new museums, which are still financed by governments, whether they are national, regional, or local.

To solve the acquisitions problem, the city museum, as with so many new museum projects, will rely on citizens to collect and donate objects. After all, it is legitimate to shape the city's collective memory by consolidating objects from individual donations to build the common cultural identity of the city. Another option is to adopt a no-collection policy, as seen in several new museum projects such as the Kyushu National Museum in Japan. Museum exhibitions then will be on a loan basis, and in this case support from other institutions will be crucial.

The City Museum and the City's Cultural Planning

As a developing state, Taiwan gave priority to economic development; its cultural programming did not begin until the late 1970s. Unlike its trajectory of economic development in the 1950s and 1960s, which was strongly backed by aid from the United States both in terms of financial support and professional expertise, Taiwan's cultural programming has been highly dynamic, and characteristically contingent on party politics and political leadership. A common trend in cultural programming since the political liberation of 1987 has been the search for local and cultural identity, which had been previously suppressed.

As the capital city, Taipei has pioneered various cultural policies and programs, among them public art programs, a scheme for the private sponsorship of art and culture, and the introduction of public-private partnerships in cultural organizations. Taipei City Museum will be the first city museum project in Taiwan and is anchored in the shaping of collective memory, cultural identity, and civic pride. The project's cultural dimension undoubtedly surpasses its economic perspective, though the latter has also been included as one policy objective.

Currently, there are more than two hundred museums and quasi-museums[13] in the city, although there is no central body in charge of the planning and development of these museums apart from a subdivision in the Department of Cultural Affairs. The city museum project can play a role in integrating other museum resources. Beyond that, because of its diverse nature, the city museum can broaden its range of concerns to embrace urban issues by engaging with different communities. However, being directly under the governance of the city government, the city museum project may run the risk of becoming part of the government's strategy to promote its policies and political agenda. It will then depend on communities, the nonprofit sector, and opposition parties to prevent a political agenda shaping the contents of the museum.

The City Museum and the Urban Planning Project: Yuan-shan Cultural Park

The city government's Department of Urban Development has proposed several urban regeneration projects to regenerate and redevelop the neighboring area around the city museum site. Of immediate concern to the museum is the Yuan-shan Cultural Park project. As the major regeneration project, it is to form a unique cluster encompassing existing cultural and leisure facilities, including an archaeological site, a children's leisure center, an art museum, a Tudor-style heritage house, two parks, a Confucian temple, a Japanese Buddhist temple built in the colonial period, a grand hotel, an observatory, a football stadium,[14] and the museum (see the aerial map of the site).

FIGURE 8.5
Map of the museum site. © Department of Cultural Affairs, Taipei
City Government.

Forming part of the proposal for the Yuan-shan Cultural Park is the
Keelung Riverside[15] regeneration project, about a fifteen-minute walk from
the museum site. Once the project is completed, the area will not only attract more visitors but also will be extended both along the river and via the
already finished citywide bicycle paths. There are at least three other projects to revitalize the Yuan-shan Cultural Park area, all of which will add
considerably to its attractiveness.

The park has several advantages to enhance further its potential distinc-
tiveness among the city's cultural and leisure amenities. First of all, the area
is environmentally friendly and ideal for developing activities with an ecological dimension—which has been one of the city government's major
policy objectives. Second, the land in the area is owned mostly by the city
government,[16] and there are no residential buildings involved, which otherwise might necessitate complicated and lengthy processes to relocate residents. Third, the area will provide a unique feature[17] with a great variety
of activities when neighboring projects are completed. As contemporary
urban leisure styles have changed to embrace a mixture of leisure and cul-

tural activities, allied to concerns with healthy lifestyles, city residents tend to seek multipurpose activities. The Yuan-shan Cultural Park, of which the museum is an integral part, will offer a unique opportunity to match such lifestyle aspirations, making the total visitor experience in this area worthwhile. Each project in the network has its own significance in contributing to the overall success of the whole area, and the museum will benefit considerably from this unique location.

CONCLUSION

Unlike culture in Western countries, which strongly maintain (in theory, if not always in practice) that culture should be as distant from politics as possible, culture in Taiwan has been heavily utilized to achieve political objectives. In spite of criticism, the practice remains strong and explicit. The fierce and sometimes vicious party political infighting in Taiwan has hindered the country's development in all respects, including cultural projects. As the capital, Taipei has been the main battleground of party politics since the late 1990s. It is hoped that the city museum project will remain as a politics-free zone in order to achieve its idea of shaping a common history, identity, and future for city residents.

Another difference, certainly from the North American experience, is that the government still plays a crucial role in the success of cultural projects. Meanwhile, the project's continuous support and endorsement from political leaders are important, as it involves a huge financial outlay. Whether the project will be economically effective is highly uncertain.

Finally, cross-departmental collaboration and public-private partnerships are important in urban planning projects. There is probably no museum project that focuses only on the experience inside the museum space itself; to facilitate the whole visiting experience, many considerations beyond this space have to be taken into account. The success of the Taipei City Museum project will rely on close collaboration among museum professionals, policy makers, and the urban planning communities.

NOTES

1. The Department of Cultural Affairs, established in 1999, is in charge of the city's cultural policies and cultural organizations.

2. F. Bianchini and M. Parkinson, *Cultural Policy and Urban Regeneration: The West European Experience* (New York: Manchester University Press, 1993); S. Miles and R. Paddison, "Introduction: The Rise and Rise of Culture-Led Urban Regeneration," *Urban Studies* 42, nos. 5–6 (2005): 833–839.

3. G. Evans, "Measure for Measure: Evaluating the Evidence of Culture's Contribution to Regeneration," *Urban Studies* 42, nos. 5–6 (2005): 959–983.

4. S. Sassen, *The Global City: New York, London, Tokyo* (Princeton, NJ: Princeton University Press, 1991).

5. Treaties of Tien-jin.

6. For a general history of Taiwan, see B. Su B., *Taiwan's 400-Year History: The Origins and Continuing Development of the Taiwanese Society and People* (Washington, DC: Taiwanese Cultural Grassroots Association, 1986); and D. Roy, *Taiwan: A Political History* (Ithaca, NY: Cornell University Press, 2003).

7. R. Y.-W. Kwok, *Globalizing Taipei: The Political Economy of Spatial Development* (New York: Routledge, 2005).

8. The department changed its name to the Department of Information and Tourism in 2007.

9. The cultural elite plays a critical role in Chinese societies. See T. A. Metzger, "The Western Concept of Civil Society in the Context of Chinese History," in *Civil Society: History and Possibilities*, ed. S. Kaviraj and S. Khilnani (Cambridge: Cambridge University Press, 2001).

10. After losing the civil war to the Communist party, the Nationalist Government, led by Chiang Kai-shek, fled to Taiwan in 1949.

11. J.-Y. Hsu, "The Evolution of Economic Base: From Industrial City, Post-Industrial City to Interface City," in *Globalizing Taipei: The Political Economy of Spatial Development*, ed. R.-Y. Kwok (New York: Routledge, 2005).

12. Academic departments, including those of urban planning, architecture, geography, history, and sociology, in various universities have contributed to the study of the city. For instance, the Department of Urban Planning at National Taiwan University is one of the pioneers engaging in the urban study of the city and community empowerment on urban issues.

13. Quasi-museums can include art and cultural centers and museums with no permanent collections.

14. The football stadium is adjacent to the museum site. Because of various design problems, the stadium has never functioned properly and it is expected to be demolished for other uses in the future.

15. Keelung River is a branch of the Tanshui River.

16. The military police headquarters, which cuts off traffic from the eastern side of the area, is not owned by city government. The heavily armed headquarters' unwelcoming and austere atmosphere deters people from getting near. If the headquarters moves somewhere else, traffic flow in this area will be greatly enhanced.

17. The different architectural styles in this area—the Grand Hotel, the Taipei Fine Arts Museum, the Taipei Story House, and the museum project—also provide a unique physical feature in the city's urban landscape.

9

Museums and Urban Renewal in Towns

MAX HEBDITCH

The fourth conference of the International Association of City Museums, which took place in Amsterdam in November 2005, was titled "City Museums as Centers of Civic Dialogue?"[1] This suggested that museums are in a good position to provide a context and a forum for debate about urban space from the perspective of history, art, and the natural environment. According to UN-HABITAT, the world population living in urban areas equaled that living in rural areas in 2007. "Living in urban areas" is often abbreviated by journalists and politicians to "living in cities," with the connotation that they are big. At Amsterdam the smallest cities talked about were Hartford in Connecticut (population 121,000) and Bruges in Belgium (population 117,000). Stavanger (population 117,000) in Norway is a European City of Culture in 2008. However, the UN definition of the world's total urban population is based on what each country chooses to define as urban. This can be population size (lower limits for "urban" range from 200 to 50,000 people) or administrative status.[2] Thus, living in a big city is actually not the urban experience of most people. They still live in towns smaller than Bruges and in villages such as those found in the South West Region of England, a surprisingly nonurbanized area in one of the most densely populated countries in the world.

114

This paper looks at four issues from the viewpoint of South West England, where I now work, and how museums can play a role in addressing them. The first two issues are:

1. Many people's urban experience is in small towns, many of which have lost their urban character.
2. The sustainability of our society in the face of climate change requires that the benefits that tempt people to work and/or live in the large city have to be spread more widely through the reurbanization of medium and small towns.

This leads to the questions raised in Venice in 2006 by the tenth international architecture exhibition, Cities: People, Society, Architecture,[3] curated by Richard Burdett: Who controls, and is democratically accountable for, the planning processes? How do we make urban spaces work in a globalized free-market world?

Prima facie, museums are very relevant to this process of urban renewal. Potential areas for museum action range from presenting a historical and ecological understanding of the small town to being players in implementing planning strategies for development. Given the strong ethical dimension to museum practice expressed in the International Council of Museums' codes, what museums say and do will always show a bias to sustainability in the face of climate change. However, the extent to which museums can engage with those who control the planning process, whether or not they are democratically accountable, is conditioned by their position within government structures and civil society. This chapter, therefore, looks mainly at leadership and management issues.

South West England is a long and relatively narrow peninsula with a surface area of 2.4 million hectares (18 percent of the UK), of which only 216,000 hectares (9 percent) is covered with buildings (see figure 9.1).[4] Its principal industries are aerospace, farming, and tourism. Of the total South West population[5] of 5,038,000, only 61 percent live in urban communities of 10,000 or more people, compared with 90 percent in the UK as a whole. Only 35 percent live in towns of 100,000 or more, compared with 60 percent for the UK (see figure 9.2).

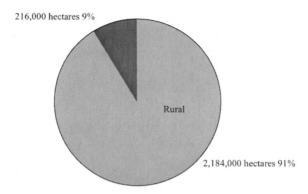

216,000 hectares 9%

Rural

2,184,000 hectares 91%

FIGURE 9.1
Area of South West England covered by buildings.

These figures emphasize the dispersed nature of population in the South West. With the exception of Bournemouth and Poole, whose communication links are with the adjoining South East region, the larger towns are mainly distributed along the corridor of the main M4 and M5 motorways and the broadly parallel main railway (see figure 9.3). Thus the urban experience of many people in the South West has been and will be in the

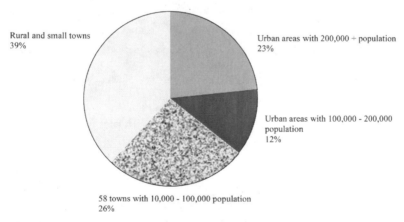

Rural and small towns
39%

Urban areas with 200,000 + population
23%

Urban areas with 100,000 - 200,000
population
12%

58 towns with 10,000 - 100,000 population
26%

FIGURE 9.2
Urban populations in South West England.

small towns outside this corridor. The urban character of those in rural areas has been ebbing since the coming of railways in the mid-nineteenth
century. From 1850 to 1930 the populations of towns in remoter areas, particularly in the west of the region, fell as agriculture, woolen industries, and
mining declined. Seaside resorts were less affected as tourism grew. Although small town populations have grown since the 1930s, greatest in
those within easy reach of the cities, in recent years centralization and globalization have led to the loss of some key elements that define the urban:
locally accountable and powerful government, magistrates (lower) courts,
small industries, livestock markets, hospitals, access to railways, and so on.
These are all concentrated in fewer centers. The compensations are often
lively communities in many towns, reflected in a plethora of small, mainly
volunteer-run museums, and broadband access to the Internet.

Considerable concern has been expressed in the media about the destruction of these "traditional market towns," as they are called. They are,
in reporter Paul Brown's words, "condemned to history."[6] He identifies the
problem as towns being crystallized by the construction of a bypass to ease
traffic congestion; the land between the town center and the new road

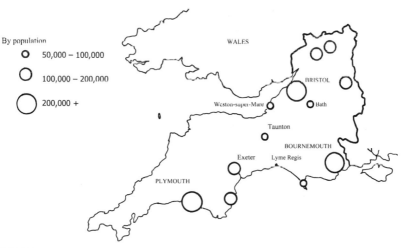

FIGURE 9.3
Principal urban areas in South West England.

being filled with housing; high street shops closing as the supermarkets take over; deindustrialization killing off small manufacturers providing jobs; employment remaining only in the service sector (including heritage); and commuting to find work and entertainment being essential. This analysis raises a major issue of importance for anywhere: If we are to reduce the use of fossil fuels in order to control global warming, one aspect of the strategy must be to reduce car use and "food miles." The opportunities for work and leisure that attract people to the big town or city have once again to be dispersed over many urban centers. In other words, the "residual value" of community life in small towns, nascent in the museum life we see in the South West, has to be nurtured and other aspects revitalized.

This brings us to issue 3: How is the process of renewal to be controlled in an accountable way? Government in England (Scotland, Wales, and Ireland have devolved governments) is highly centralized in London. Local councils have relatively little discretion in what they can do and are mainly accountable for providing services prescribed and paid for by central government. There is no democratically elected regional authority for South West England, but a number of appointed regional government agencies have a powerful role in planning and economic development. At a local level, each council is guided in its planning and spending choices by a local strategic partnership, on which are represented the police, health services, education, business, and sometimes culture. There is a strong requirement on strategic partnerships to involve ordinary people in these choices.

Because museums are weak organizations with multiple stakeholders, what they can achieve in this structure is contingent on the political, economic, social, and geographical circumstances in which they find themselves. Museums need to take advantage of any favorable winds that are blowing in public policy. In this respect, museums in South West England have some things going for them: The need for urban regeneration is recognized in two major policies produced by the regional governmental agencies:

- The Regional Spatial Strategy sees larger towns as hubs of economic growth. Out of this have emerged action plans for urban renewal, with great emphasis on environmental sustainability.[7]

- The Market and Coastal Towns Initiative, although it does not provide new infrastructure or businesses, does provide grants to enable the elected town council, working with local businesses, schools, police, and community organizations, to produce an action plan showing how their small town should develop.[8]

However, the extent to which museums can do things depends very much on the degree of autonomy they have in conducting their affairs, the quality of their leadership and management, what sort of town they are in, and if they are located where the regional governmental agencies want to encourage investment. This is an opportunist game in free-market Britain. Let us look at three examples.

TAUNTON

Taunton (population 58,241) is the capital of the county of Somerset and a middle-size town.[9] Investment is needed in the Museum of Somerset in Taunton Castle to remedy a long period of under-resourcing. It is taking advantage of the Regional Spatial Strategy. This proposes that, with its nearby twin town of Bridgwater, Taunton should be expanded and regenerated to become the focus of what will be in effect a new city-region between Exeter and Bristol. For the museum to take advantage of this, it was necessary to think about issue 4: How do we make urban spaces work, what is needed culturally in this respect, and what could be the cultural contribution to establishing a town's competitive position in a globalized world? The approach was to link with other cultural organizations, sport, education, and business to advocate a "culture-led" approach to regeneration. The museum became an actor in the development process by being part of an informal organization known as the Taunton Cultural Consortium (which I chair). The consortium advises property developers and public authorities in the sort of language they understand:

- We demonstrated the contribution of culture, including sport, to society and the economy[10]:
  - One job is created outside a cultural organization for every two inside

- Cultural venues in Taunton provide outlets for the creative industries (audiovisual, performance, publishing, arts and crafts), which employ around 6,000 people in the surrounding area (2.5 percent of its total workforce)
- The presence of museums, concert halls, and theaters helps attract the ablest people to live in the town and contribute to its economy
- We showed that there are new audiences for the three main organizations (museum, theater and arts center, and sports ground) provided that the quality of their buildings and programming meets their expectations. Otherwise people will use the motorway to go to the bigger cities of Exeter or Bristol.
- We stated that if investment in cultural infrastructure is to have an impact, it needs to be concentrated in a "cultural quarter" in the historic center of town, with high standards of urban design in the public spaces linking its elements.

This approach has begun to pay off. Regeneration of Taunton is culture- and sustainability-led. Funding is in place and work has started. Private-sector funding will rebuild the sports ground as a space that can also be used for large events such as pop concerts. A feasibility study is in progress for increasing the size of the auditoriums and providing a new art gallery in the Theater and Arts Center. A multi-million-pound grant from the Heritage Lottery Fund will renew the Museum of Somerset. The keys to this success seem to be these:

- Although the Museum of Somerset is part of the County Council, its significance as a cultural actor in regenerating Taunton is recognized at a political level, and it has been able to operate with some independence.
- The museum raised its current game, without waiting for the future, with a series of exhibitions and events with which people engaged immediately.
- The independently chaired Taunton Cultural Consortium provides a powerful voice for culture, even though it has no resources of its own, because it is prepared to understand and enlist in its mission the world outside museums and culture.

WESTON-SUPER-MARE

By contrast, North Somerset Museum at Weston-super-Mare (population: 80,076) has been given much less weight in urban renewal. The town is one of two large towns in the city-region focused on Bristol (population 551,056), the other being the World Heritage Site City of Bath (population 90,144). Weston's economy was originally founded on tourism, which dates back to the nineteenth century.[11] But as a resort in which to spend a holiday, it is now unable to compete with warmer climates. Unlike Taunton, which is more separate, Weston-super-Mare has become linked economically and socially with Bristol; it is part of a local authority on the edge of Bristol embracing other towns and countryside. Examination of some of Weston's urban renewal identified some major issues to be addressed in finding a new role for the town:[12]

- There are significant pockets of deprivation using the government's standard indices.[13]
- There is considerable inward migration by those over age 65, placing demands on social services.
- The reduction in long-stay holiday makers has led to overprovision of accommodation and a lowering of prices and quality. This has led to visitor accommodation being converted to housing.
- Employment is weighted to distribution, the remaining hotels, and restaurants. Manufacturing has declined and is now relatively unimportant.
- Of the 50,000 economically active people in Weston, 3,500 (7 percent) commute to Bristol each day.

The strategy for tackling these problems adopted by North Somerset Council, the relevant council for the town, with the support of the Regional Development Agency is to strengthen the economic base of the town by increasing its self-containment through more employment, thus reducing commuting to nearby Bristol.[14] However, only now is culture beginning to be seen as a component in the town's renewal and regeneration.[15] There is as yet no umbrella body for culture, as in Taunton, to press its importance for Weston's society and economy.

North Somerset Museum, located in the town, is very low down in the administrative hierarchy of North Somerset Council and hampered by lack of resources. The museum has secured small grants for some interesting projects. It compensates for its lowly position in the local government bureaucracy by working with people and communities in a critical way. A recent success story is an exhibition on teenage life since the 1950s (when teenage life is said to have begun), which was researched, developed, and displayed by working with youth groups in the town, without compromising the necessary curatorial authority of the museum. The project enabled individual young people to mature over the two years the project took. It was shortlisted for a national award.[16] The next project is looking at inward migration, most of which is from London and the south east, by recording and presenting individual stories. Both projects have a strong connection

FIGURE 9.4
An exhibition on teenage life at the museum in Weston-super-Mare, developed with local youth groups. © Max Hebditch.

with what is happening in towns in South West England generally and directly inform debate about their renewal. Within the resources available at the museum and given the lack of an integrated cultural strategy for the town, this small-scale approach is probably as much as can be achieved in a town that has still to form a clear view of what it wants to be and how to make its urban spaces work.

LYME REGIS

As we have seen, there are many very small towns in South West England. Because of tourism, those which are coastal resorts continue to flourish. One such is Lyme Regis (population 4,406) on the south coast.[17] Yet it faces the same problems as most seaside towns:[18] the special needs of people retiring to these places (43.5 percent of the people are over age 60); people who live and work elsewhere owning second homes (in some parts of the town 30 percent of the homes are second homes or holiday rentals); the seasonal nature of much employment; and expensive housing (40 percent above the national average).

Lyme Regis has been trying to put the Market and Coastal Towns Initiative into practice by developing its community action plan. Its key aspirations are:

- Preserving the unique character of a place that "arouses such strong passions"
- Mixing ages and skills in a viable community through housing, employment, and leisure opportunities
- Recognizing that "our location and reliance on tourism make us very aware of the challenges of global warming" (Lyme is on inherently unstable geology and trying to fall into the sea) and turning that concern to its economic advantage

Lyme's economy is tourism- and leisure-based, with a small amount of inshore fishing. The aim is to extend the tourist season by increasing the number of midseason visitors, for whom the attraction is not the beach and water sports but walking, visiting historic monuments, the arts, food, and education. The museum has no problem in buying into this agenda for change. Regeneration is to be culture-led by three major projects currently in the planning stage: an extension of the museum, a rebuilt theater, and a residential field study center for students of all ages. One advantage of a very small community is that the objectives of regeneration, and the part each including the museum can play in it, are clear to all. All the cultural actors have no alternative but to work in partnership with each other. Unfortunately, the extent to which these objectives are achievable depends on the urban and cultural regeneration priorities of much bigger regional players: the Regional Development Agency, government cultural agencies (including the national lottery distributors who have provided much funding for cultural projects over recent years), third sector organizations, and the private business sector. Not all of this is yet in place.

Lyme Regis Museum, of which I am a trustee, is a small institution with a turnover of around £80,000 each year.[19] It has a very small paid professional staff and about sixty volunteers who open the museum to the public and assist in curation and education. The planned extension will provide it with the infrastructure necessary for a modern museum: education spaces, access to collections, temporary exhibition galleries, and so forth. It has no difficulty in demonstrating its contribution to the economy in the same way as the museum in Taunton. When extended, it will provide 5.6 jobs inside and outside the museum and contribute about £140,000 gross value to the general Lyme economy. In museum terms, we play a unique part in widening people's understanding of Lyme, most obviously its geology, and in showing how the exciting development of the earth sciences in this area in the early nineteenth century took place in the context of Lyme's emergence as a resort town. The future extension will be a demonstration of sustainable building construction and management as an exemplar that others can follow. This will include energy-saving construction methods, solar panels, and wind turbines—the museum is right on the edge of the sea.

Thus within the limitations of a very small town that still retains a strong urban character, it is possible for its museum to cover big themes such as the origins of the earth sciences, to be a component in making the town a good place to live and work in as well as visit, and to do so in a way that is environmentally sustainable.

CONCLUSION

This chapter was inspired by thinking about how museums could act in relation to the issues raised by the Venice exhibition in 2006, which concentrated on a handful of megacities. But my recent work in South West England indicates that many people's experience of the urban is in small towns in a region that is still predominantly rural. If this is true of other parts of the world, our experience here may have some resonances in formulating museum policy.

However, many small towns have been diminished as the institutions of civic identity (law courts, local government, etc.) have been taken away through government centralization, local factories have closed, and agriculture has declined. To some extent this has been compensated by the continued growth of civil society (clubs and local history museums) and an increasing number of creative industries. Even middle-size towns such as Taunton find themselves as elements of larger units of local government. Those that, like Weston-super-Mare, are within the orbit of larger towns have seen their function become that of suburbanized dormitories for commuters.

It is clear that if we are to make urban spaces work, then it has to be all urban spaces. Car use has to go down. All towns must have economic autonomy in terms of jobs. Leisure and learning opportunities have to be provided in all towns, for their own citizens and for those living in the adjoining villages. Civic action has to be delivered by civil society as well as by the institutions of government.

Museums have a part to play in this, most obviously in recording and transmitting an understanding of urban historical change in the environment, human behavior, and migration. However, the three case studies I have used show that museums with urban collections can or could do much more than this. Given leadership, they can become actors in the processes of urban renewal and regeneration. This requires the museum to identify the wider agendas at work in government and society. In South

West England, the Regional Spatial Framework for planning development provides the overall picture. Local Strategic Partnerships provide a mechanism within which museums can act. In relation to these agendas, it is not enough simply to state that museums are a good thing; the indirect benefits to the economy, social cohesion, and education have to be stated as well, as we have seen in Lyme Regis and Taunton. It is also important that museums operating in this context do so in conjunction with other cultural players, such as theaters, libraries, and sports facilities. We are all in this together.

However, of the three case studies I have described, while the museums in Taunton and Lyme Regis are able to work these systems, the one in Weston-super-Mare is having more difficulty, despite some interesting programming at the operational level. Although the objective of Weston's renewal is clear—to make the town less dependent on Bristol—the part its museum could play in this is less developed. The difference may be that the museums in Lyme Regis and Taunton have a greater degree of independence, whereas in Weston-super-Mare the museum is almost lost in the local government bureaucracy. Getting museum governance and structures right is still work in progress.

NOTES

1. R. Kistemaker, ed., *City Museums as Centers of Civic Dialogue? Proceedings of the Fourth Conference of the International Association of City Museums, 3–5 November 2005* (Amsterdam: Amsterdam Historical Museum, 2006).

2. United Nations Department of Economic and Social Affairs, Population Division, *World Urbanization Prospects: The 2001 Revision* (New York: United Nations Publications, 2001), 106. There are two official definitions of "urban" in the United Kingdom: "an urban area is an extent of at least 20 hectares and at least 1,500 residents" (UK Office of National Statistics) and "settlements with a population of 10,000 or more" (UK Department of Communities and Local Government). Contemporary urban character, something more than an official agglomeration of an arbitrary number of people, is difficult to define but usually recognizable. For a museum understanding, see M. Hebditch, "Museums about Cities," *Museum International* no. 187, vol. 47, no. 3 (July–September 1995): 7–11.

3. R. Burdett and S. Ichioka, *Cities: People, Society, Architecture* (Venice: Marsilio Editori, 2006).

4. *The Generalized Land Use Database* (London: ODPM, 2005) contains experimental statistics for land use in the English regions and has been produced for 2001.

5. Population figures throughout are drawn from Office of National Statistics, *Key Statistics for Urban Areas in the South West and Wales* (London: HMSO, 2004). These are based on the 2001 census.

6. See *Guardian*, February 7, 2007.

7. *Draft Regional Spatial Strategy for the South West*, Taunton, SW Regional Assembly, 2006. www.southwest-ra.gov.uk.

8. See www.southwestrda.org.uk/what-we-do/regeneration/market-towns.

9. For a general account of the history of Taunton, see T. Mayberry, *The Vale of Taunton Past* (Chichester: Phillimore, 1998).

10. Sources: S. Brand and E. McVittie, *Economic Contribution of Museums, Libraries and Galleries in the South West* (Taunton: SWMLAC, 2004); Colin Mercer, *Making a Difference* (Taunton: SWMLAC, 2004); S. Brand and E. McVittie, *Economic Contribution of Museums and Galleries in the South West* (Taunton: SWMLAC, 2004); D. Shellard, *Economic Impact Study of UK Theater* (London: Arts Council England and others, 2004); Arts and Business, *Private Investment in the Arts* (2002–2003); DCMS, *Creative Industries Mapping Document* (London: DCMS, 2001); Stuart Davies, *Regeneration and Renewal in the South West* (Taunton: SWMLAC, 2004); Bill Ferguson, *Harnessing Opportunities: A Strategy for the Creative Industries in Somerset* (Integria, 2004). See also G. Evans and P. Shaw, *The Contribution of Culture to Regeneration in the UK: A Review of the Evidence* (London: DCMS, 2004).

11. For a summary history of the town, see S. Poole, *History and Guide: Weston-super-Mare* (Stroud: Tempus, 2002).

12. ARUP, *Weston Area Action Plan: Socio Economic Report* (Weston-super-Mare: North Somerset Council, 2005); *Topic Paper: Culture, Leisure and Tourism* (Weston-super-Mare: North Somerset Council, 2007), par. 3.10.

13. These include such things as housing, living environment, health, and disability.

14. *Draft Regional Spatial Strategy for the South West* (Taunton: SW Regional Assembly, 2006), par. 4.2.20–4.2.23.

15. *Topic Paper: Culture, Leisure and Tourism*, par. 3.10. For access to this and other papers see www.n-somerset.gov.uk and follow links.

16. See www.n-somerset.gov.uk/museum.

17. For a general account of Lyme Regis see J. Fowles, *A Short History of Lyme Regis* (Wimborne: Dovecote Press, 1991). For the World Heritage Site and the origins of geology in Lyme see Dorset County Council, *Nomination of the Dorset and East Devon Coast for Inclusion in the World Heritage List* (Dorchester: Dorset County Council, 2000).

18. Lyme Regis Development Trust, *Lyme Forward* (Lyme Regis: LRDT, 2007).

19. See www.lymeregismuseum.co.uk.

10

The Development of the City of Kazan

The Museum Aspect

GULCHACHAK RAKHIMZYANOVNA NAZIPOVA

Kazan, the capital of the Republic of Tatarstan, is one of Russia's largest cities and one of the most dynamic. In recent years the city has been developing at a rapid pace, and the result has been the opening of a string of cultural, scientific, educational, and entertainment centers. Existing cultural facilities are flourishing: theaters are getting a new impetus; concerts are held more often; and international festivals, such as the opera festival named after Chaliapin (who was born in Kazan), the ballet festival named in honor of Nureyev, and a festival of Muslim films, have become regular features of the cultural scene. In short, Kazan is turning into a large, modern city.

This chapter considers the place of museums in the development of Kazan, which is a large regional museum center. There are more than two hundred museums in the city—large and small, state, departmental, school, and university museums—all of which are important keepers of the historical and cultural heritage of the people of this multinational region. However, even though new museums are established and new exhibitions are opened in Kazan every year, they are far from being a natural part of city life. Although the number of visitors grows noticeably from year to year, going to a museum is not a regular habit for the majority. As everywhere, going to the museum is just one of very many activities competing for people's attention. In practice, popular entertainment from football to fitness clubs, discos, and the cinema play a more significant part in the lives of Kazaners.

Much of the problem can be put down to the popular view of museums as places of silence, isolated from the world around them, backward in terms of the technical innovation that has become commonplace in people's everyday lives, and not very accessible to ordinary people. Therefore there is a barrier to overcome in communicating the heritage of the city to its citizens. It is a situation that needs some analysis and a solution, as the museum as an active social institution can play a significant part in the city's development.

There are a number of reasons for this situation. Unquestionably, the most important are the sociopolitical and economic upheavals in Russia over the last few years, which have served to destabilize social and cultural life. But there are more concrete reasons connected directly to the museum as an institution.

The National Museum of Tatarstan is the biggest museum in Kazan. Close connection between the museum and the city has always been of the greatest importance. Indeed, when it was originally set up it was called the Kazan City Museum. Interestingly, one of the museum's founders was the mayor, S. V. Dyachenko. As a free, democratic, and open institution the museum played an important role in collecting material on the city and in reaching out to the population. The statutes of 1894 enlarged the museum's mission to take in economic and industrial concerns, with the aim to "aid in the development of local industry by showing the best examples." Over the years, priorities, naturally, changed and other aims and specific objectives came to the fore. From the middle of the twentieth century and up to the 1980s, the museum was an attractive place to visit, to learn something, or simply to meet up with friends. Frequently an interesting exhibition would bring in large numbers of people.

However, times changed and some specific factors contributed to a decline in visitor numbers. To begin with, there was a fire in 1987. It did not destroy the collections, but exhibitions had to be dismantled and the clear impression was given that the museum had closed. Then matters were made worse by the deepening economic and social crisis that gripped the country. Of course, the museum was not alone in going through a bad patch—throughout the 1990s, museums across Russia lost visitors. Yet somehow the museum not only survived but managed to maintain and even increase its funding, continue its exhibition program, and keep together its core of museum professionals. At the time of this writing, damage to the building has been repaired and the galleries have been upgraded to meet current requirements.

For 112 years, the role of the museum has been fundamental to the work of museums in the city. It has a collection of more that 800,000 artifacts, covering regional and city history from the beginnings up to the present, including some rare items of natural history. But is this rich inheritance of any interest to locals? Statistics demonstrate that visitor numbers to all Kazan's museums including the National Museum still remain insignificant, in spite of the fact that the collections are unique, of national (let alone local) importance, and public property: they belong to the public.

A different approach is needed to attract the differing segments of visitors. As matters stand, most visitors are schoolchildren. It is not that they are particularly interested in museums; they are brought to museums by their teachers, a requirement of the city authorities. At the same time the museum resorts to ways of motivating both the children and their teachers—for example, organizing competitions to raise interest and awareness of the exhibitions with a prize for the winner. It is something taken up by other museums in the city. This sort of approach can help make a museum visit not only a compulsory part of the school curriculum, but one to look forward to.

It is equally important to create a positive and attractive image to welcome museum visitors. Traditional forms of museum activity such as lectures and excursions have been supplemented by new ones such as interactive role plays, dramatized educational classes, or classes about costumes. Then there are the museum clubs. There are a number at the museum—Chronos, for example, for children who are interested in archaeology, and an embroidery and fashion club for girls who like needle-work.

One club in particular is unique and has become part of city life. The Vityas club involves groups of teenagers in historical and military recon-structions and role plays; the club manager, V. V. Khabarov, has become a respected figure among them. Mention should be made also of the mu-seum children's summer camp, where more than a hundred children have their break every year. Children are immersed in particular periods in his-tory, and more than fifteen workshops make their holiday on the banks of the ancient River Kama on the site of the medieval town of Kashan both in-teresting and entertaining. Closely connected to the museum world, these activities become the basis for children and teenagers to learn about the history of their motherland and to encourage them to return to the mu-seum again and again, creating a bond that can last into their adult lives.

Another project is "A Night in the Museum." Its main aim is to target young clubbers or young people out on the streets at night and get them into the museum. We have achieved some success—a small but important victory in giving young people a different perspective on how they could spend their leisure time.

However, there remains the crucial matter of enticing back the adult vis-itor. The most stable group are the retired who have kept up the habit of museum visiting. Then there are the history students, teachers, and univer-sity academics, especially in the humanities. They come back time and again to look up documents or work in the library; they bring their stu-dents with them; they take part in conferences, seminars, and discussions. To them the museum remains an indispensable part of their professional life.

Nevertheless, broadening the adult visitor base is a constant concern. There is a tendency among most city people to feel that the way they live in a contemporary, dynamic society does not leave much time for visiting an exhibition, especially when they are presented with such a wide range of choices for spending their leisure time. When they do have the time avail-able, the museum is not high on their list of priorities. The first attempt to overcome this attitude was setting aside evenings for businesspeople. In particular, the museum organized an exhibition dedicated to the anniversary of the largest company in Tatarstan, the Tatenergo Power Company, and invited the current administration and former employees. Most of those present admitted that they had either never been to a museum or had not been for a very long time, and if it were not for this particular occasion directly connected with their professional life, they would not have bothered to visit. However, they left with the intention not only of coming back, but also of bringing their families with them.

One more example in this direction concerned the city elite and their guests, when the museum organized a reception during the annual meeting of the European Bank for Reconstruction and Development, held in Kazan. Museum guests could continue chatting with their colleagues while at the same time following a dramatized presentation of the museum's permanent collection, including some unique objects in the collection and the history of Tatarstan and Kazan.

Another way of getting people in through the museum's doors is to mount exhibitions that have impact on the city's cultural life and have a wide appeal beyond the immediate confines of the museum world. In 2005 the large-scale project Museum Rarities: The City's One-Thousandth Anniversary reverberated across the city. In 2007 a string of new exhibitions was held for specific interest groups: theater lovers had Theater Magic, ecologists and hunters had The Call of Ancestors, and The World of Musical Instruments was targeted at musicians and ethnographers. Each of these projects became a memorable event in the cultural calendar of the city.

It has become an almost universal truth that to have wide appeal a museum needs to welcome visitors with a shop, a restaurant or a café, and perhaps a recreation zone, all of which can bear comparison with the best of commercial practice and provide an agreeable introduction to historical and cultural heritage.

To this same end, information technology festivals and exhibitions incorporating state-of-the-art technology, including computer games, can help overcome the stereotypical view of museums as rather obsolete and therefore not very interesting places. Several adult visitors commented favorably on the computer games on the ancient history of Tatarstan, which attracted the attention of their children and motivated them to come to the museum again.

So far, few tourists visit the city's museums. Yet the development of the city and its museums cannot be fully achieved without tourism. Tourism, whether from abroad or from within Russia, is developing slowly, not least due to the upheavals of recent history. Yet the situation is changing. A city like Kazan, which celebrated its millennium in 2005, cannot help being attractive for tourists, and the city's museums are getting actively involved in attracting tourists. In April 2007 for the first time museums were featured at a tourism industry gathering, and tour operators were presented with tourist routes including the participation of museums. It goes without saying that museums in Tatarstan are noncommercial institutions. However, getting and keeping the income they earn from tourists or any other source, an income that will allow them to maintain their standards and develop, remain important. The museum remains optimistic—one project, Music of the Museum, won the V. Potanin grant in the Changing Museum in the Changing World competition in 2006, and the museum succeeded in attracting financial support from business partners to implement joint exhibition projects. Other museums of the city are also looking for similar ways of finding their place in the city landscape; a variety of projects, large and small, are taking place to activate and enliven city museums.

The problems faced by Kazan's museums are typical of those faced across Russia. They are a consequence of radical changes in the country and the transition to a market economy. New economic conditions make it difficult to implement the systematic maintenance of artifacts and to carry out restoration work. Setting up new exhibitions requires a considerable financial outlay and technical support. That is why the further development of the museum is possible only on the basis of strategic planning and the prioritizing of tasks at every stage.

The museum has prepared a long-term development program, which will make it possible to incorporate its accumulated experience into a working system to carry out practical measures to develop an investment policy. For example, in the heart of Kazan a research and information center, unique in Russia, has been created on all aspects of museum activities.

To bring the project to life the museum has set up a Museum Friends Club; prepared a business plan; and asked city residents to become sponsors, investors, and partners.

Museums need to become an inseparable and necessary part of the ever-changing city. By collecting and preserving the city's historical and cultural heritage, they are contributing to the development of the city and the wider region. In so doing they are able to influence city development in ways that are positive and rewarding.

11

Defining a Research Agenda for City Museums in a Peripheralizing World

GEOFFREY EDWARDS AND MARIE LOUISE BOURBEAU

Museums of the city form a world apart. Most museums are defined by their collections, whether these be archaeological, artistic, scientific, or some eclectic form of artifact. City museums are different—although many also manage collections, they are not defined by these collections, but rather by the city's spaces. A city museum may have no collection at all, aside from the living arrangements in the city itself, which form a special kind of collection, *extra muros*. Indeed, new city museums understand this point directly. They are more committed to exploring intangibles. Many are opening even their design activities to public participation in more direct and interactive ways. They are becoming porous, more attentive to the mood of our times, more engaged in a process of circulation of modes of being.

City museums form a group unto themselves, with an agenda that is still unfolding. This shift in identity and purpose has profound implications for all museums—indeed, for all forms of cultural expression and memory.

This chapter sets out ten thematic areas that form, collectively, a kind of road map for the research and development agenda for museums of cities. Each of these thematic areas is presented in sequence, along with supporting material. However, this material is introduced via a brief overview of the changing socioeconomic context of our time.

A PERIPHERALIZING WORLD

The September 2005 edition of *Scientific American* was devoted to a status report about the world's population. Here, laid out clearly in print, was the observation that, for the first time in human history, the global rate of growth of the world's population was dropping. A variety of studies support this observation—indeed, it has become apparent that the population growth rate peaked in the mid-1960s, and has dropped by half since then.[1]

This is a hugely important observation. As long as the world was functioning with a population dynamic characterized by exponential growth, the population engine acted as a driver for a vast array of economic and social processes. When the impetus stopped, these processes changed, and the world has been reconfiguring itself ever since.

The ubiquitous understanding of economic growth as a stimulant for improved quality of life is a consequence of our modern theories of economic growth, which have been developed during times of high population growth. Although not all economic theories link economic growth positively to population growth,[2] as the population flattens out over the coming decades, it is widely expected that economic growth will slow.[3]

The existence of large groupings of people with similar background and culture also derives from high population growth; when populations grow rapidly, they cluster into homogeneous regions,[4] unless a strong mixing function is in play. The existence of national boundaries also follows from high population growth. Nations came into being at least partially as a result of population expansion and competition between neighboring regions;[5] the modern notion of a nation-state associates the political entity of the state with the geographic and cultural entity of a nation.

The centralization of economic and social power into institutions follows from rapid population growth. In an expanding economy, power tends to accumulate in the center, and institutions are created to hold and nurture this power.

When the pump that drives population growth stopped, these processes fell into decline: that part of economic growth driven by population growth, the tendency toward the formation of homogeneous clusters with a well-defined core, the ongoing maintenance of national borders, and the centralization of social and economic power—all began to lose their hold. As a result, we call the new socioeconomic dynamics a process of "peripheralization."

While the current time of transition is hard to describe, because it mixes the past processes with new ones, the convergent state toward which we as a global society are moving is easier to characterize, at least in some regards. In four small words, first stated by the Irish poet W. B. Yeats, "The center cannot hold." The world that is coming into being will be characterized by more heterogeneous sociocultural mixing; over time, the large homogeneous groups that still make up much of the world will break up. At the same time, the boundaries that separated these homogeneous groups from each other—national borders, cultural prejudices, and so on—will dissipate. Centralized institutions, including museums, will begin to reform into different arrangements. Like today's corporations, which are becoming virtual entities spread across the globe, institutions will become more distributed and diffuse; will adopt a horizontal, networked structure; and will fragment spatially into different locations. Economic growth will slow and change form. Instead of continuously expanding the production of quantities, we shall see a shift to producing improved quality, and a broadening of our economy from purely monetary considerations to other social, cultural, and even spiritual values such as the green values.

Already, we see evidence of such changes. The whole process has been enabled by what Thomas Friedman calls the "flattening of the world,"[6] a change in culture that Friedman attributes to the emergence of the Internet. By flattening, Friedman is referring to the tendency to equalize access to each other across the planet, hence to the elimination of boundaries and barriers. The population argument we put forward, however, suggests that the Internet itself may have arisen as a result of or in parallel with other forces already in play.

We call this process the "peripheralization of the world," a somewhat different emphasis than that of Friedman. The periphery is no longer "out there," but rather, it is all around us. What used to be called centers are now "nodes" or "intersections," places where information or forces come together, and they are often temporary.

The citification of the world is part of this process of peripheralization. As the hinterland disappears, the world becomes city, and the collection of cities forms its own periphery. City museums participate in this change. Just as cities must learn to exchange and share information and experiences across the network of city spaces, so the network of city museums must learn to act together within this new space.

Another important consequence of these changing socio-demographic dynamics is their impact on the experience of personal and group identity. When individuals functioned within homogeneous cultural environments with well-defined boundaries, identity was understood to be unitary—that is, a person had one identity, and that identity was exclusive of all others. In today's world, this is no longer the case. Increasingly, we view ourselves as having many different identities, and these do not necessarily always form a consistent whole.

In addition, the Internet forms an enabling substrate to the process of peripheralization and each mutually reinforces the other. Indeed, the Internet itself acts as a kind of global metacity, a city that connects all cities, and therefore ensures that the networked space is oiled and greased to work as a single unit. City museums must learn to operate as much in the virtual world as they do in the physical one if they are to flourish during the coming period.

THE RESEARCH AGENDA FOR CITY MUSEUMS

This discussion sets the stage for outlining a research agenda for city museums for the coming years. We have combined our own insights with those brought up in discussion with colleagues and museum specialists, to generate the following list of ten thematic areas that should be addressed.

1. Cities and Their Socioeconomic Context

The understanding of city museums must be grounded in the awareness that cities are reemerging in the twenty-first century as a viable and stable economic unit, while the nation-state is losing its political and economic hold on the world. Although contemporary cities do not resemble their medieval counterparts, they are regaining their medieval status as independent trading centers within larger economic associations, which are slowly replacing nation-states.

It has been mentioned in other chapters in this book that in 2007, for the first time in human history, more than 50 percent of the world's population lived in cities. By 2050, it is projected that the number may rise above 80 percent. The countryside is emptying out, as rural populations seek a better life within the cities. The world's largest cities are growing by leaps and bounds through the arrival of immigrants from around the world, especially from its poorer neighborhoods. As a result, the populations of such large cities are also changing—they are becoming more heterogeneous, more culturally mixed than during the twentieth century.

At the same time, although the rate of growth of the world's population has begun to decline, the population is still increasing at a high rate. To meet the influx of new population, mostly in the developing world, it is said that one new city must be created each day.[7] As a result, large cities are becoming huge metropolises, smaller cities are become large, and nascent cities are also developing. Georges Prévélakis, in his contribution to this book on the geopolitics of cities, highlights additional changes among these cities (see chapter 2).

It has been argued that the existence of nations has skewed city development, favoring one city over all others within most nations and causing other large cities within a nation to decline.[8] The root of this idea is that most economic renewal comes from the process of export replacement within cities, and that each city has its own natural cycle of economic growth. National currencies and trade agreements usually favor one city's development over all others within political units in this regard—that is to say, they are tuned to support one cycle of economic growth, usually that of the dominant city. Interest rates, for example, are often changed as a function of that city's needs, although the timing of such changes may be detrimental to other cities within the country. The emergence of larger economic regions containing several nations levels the playing field, allowing cities to develop as a function of their individual strengths. Hence within the European Union, Marseille and Lyon are no longer as disadvantaged with regard to Paris as they were, and Hamburg and Munich are less subservient to Berlin.

With the reduction in rural populations, although cities are gaining power, they may no longer have a "kingdom" over which they hold sway; instead, the world is becoming citified. In such a world, there is no effective hinterland, and hence these are not city-states as in olden times, but rather "cities unto themselves." In the absence of an effective hinterland, cities are no longer centers; rather, they are becoming the whole of the inhabited landscape. Hence we call this a process of peripheralization—that is, the collection of all cities forms a kind of periphery. Periphery is becoming more important than center. This state is exacerbated and reinforced by the existence of planetwide networks that also lack clearly defined centers—that is, by the global process of peripheralization described above.

As more and more of a nation's life passes through its cities, the latter become more complex, more interconnected, and more complete. At one time, one could encapsulate the study of cities via disciplines such as "urban studies" or "urban geography"; today, this is no longer possible. To understand cities today requires a multitude of disciplines working together and collaborating—otherwise, there is no chance of understanding the changes that are in progress.

City museums must situate their mission and goals within the context of twenty-first-century cities, whether large or small. Within a time of change, cities need a memory of their earlier states of being, and a city museum can play such a role. But cities also need to explore their new identity, to understand better where they are going (see section 3 below), and city museums are called upon to play an active role in helping this to occur.

Indeed, in the emerging network of cities, it can be argued that a city museum plays a critically important role, and one that is far more active than those that are usually attributed to museums. Although city museums may still carry out relatively passive tasks of storing and preserving collective memories of the city's past, they are strategically situated to play a more active role in the creation and management of the twenty-first-century city. They are also uniquely situated to network with other city museums across the world and to support their home city's own networking efforts (see section 9 below). Finally, city museums need to work with universities and research centers of many different disciplines to enhance their understanding of twenty-first-century cities and the unique situation of the city museum in such a context.

2. City Museums: Theoretical Underpinnings

Given that city museums may, eventually, not exploit collections in any traditional sense or be defined in terms of their collections, it becomes doubly important that they focus their studies on the emerging nature of twenty-first-century cities. What does it mean to replace the management of a collection of objects with the management of information about a city's structure and function? What does this shift in focus signify for a museum's internal structure, organization, mission, and global vision? How can the city museum help bridge the gap between the city's past and its future across a rapidly changing present?

Ivo Maroevic described museology as concerned with "the expression, valorization and affirmation of various forms of identity."[9] There are several "hot topics" in contemporary museology; there are also significant gaps where theory is lacking. Current interest focuses on understanding the museum as embodying a process of transmission of culture across generations and on evaluating the impact of a museum's organization on its public, yet very little is presented or published on modern cognition and learning theory in relation to the museum experience. Addressing this issue should help provide a stronger theoretical foundation for museums and museum schools. As the role of museums changes and their numbers rise, there is a growing need for the development and consolidation of museum schools. The Laboratoire de Muséologie et d'Ingénierie Culturelle (LAMIC) at Laval University, Canada, represents an example of such a new training environment. This facility combines state-of-the-art virtual and augmented reality technologies and digitizing instruments to present a new facet of museum studies to the next generation of students of museology. Laval University is currently undergoing a reform to better situate the museology program with regard to the challenges of museums in today's world.

As our experience of identity is changing, a variety of groups are addressing this issue, including several online communities.[10] As a result, there is an increasing focus on the multiplicity of identity as it relates to embodiment issues. This fertile area needs to be situated within the development of museum studies and museology.

3. Rethinking the Future of Cities

City museums increasingly play an active role in rethinking the future of cities. Such a process may involve forecasting and backcasting, scenario development and visioning activities, strategic planning, and various forms of community engagement. Chet Orloff (see chapter 3) highlights the role that city museums can play in urban development, especially via a process of interfacing and exchanging with municipal authorities.

Within the city of the twenty-first century, a very different landscape is emerging to that prevalent during the twentieth century. Cities today are experiencing an influx of inhabitants and cultures from other parts of the world. For example, in Canada, in the 2001 census, 14 percent of the country's population was what are called "visible minorities." By 2016, this is expected to increase to 20 percent, hence to increase by half again what it was in the year 2000,[11] and there is no suggestion that this rate of increase will slow down. Other parts of the world are experiencing similar rates of growth in the immigrant population. For example, a study in the Netherlands suggests that the "foreign" population of the four big Dutch cities (Amsterdam, Rotterdam, Utrecht, and The Hague) will exceed 50 percent in a few years.[12] Toronto today is already in this situation.

Likewise, the so-called disabled population is growing, from 12–15 percent of the total population in 1991 to over 20 percent projected by 2026 within Canada,[13] with the rate still climbing. Similar percentages seem to prevail in the United States.[14] In Australia, the population of the disabled is expected to reach about 25 percent by 2026.[15] Sociologist Irving Zola noted that disability represents "a set of characteristics everyone shares to varying degrees."[16] Within a life course perspective—that is, over the lifetime of an individual—disability affects all of us.

Related to the rise in the disabled population is the increase in the numbers of the elderly. In the developed countries, this is expected to rise from its current level of about 20 percent to more than 33 percent by 2050. In the developing countries, the level will also rise, from its current average level of about 8 percent to more than 20 percent. Overall, the fraction of the population that is elderly will increase over current levels by more than a factor of three.[17] This belies the commonly held belief that the aging of the population is a uniquely Western demographic. This is a worldwide phenomenon likely to have a huge impact on how we organize and live in our cities.

Not only will cities be more heterogeneous in terms of multiculturalism and multiethnic participation in various levels of city life, but cities must also become more human, more caring, than they have been over much of the twentieth century. It has been noted that city departments such as the police or the fire service increasingly work with other professions[18] to ensure that cities become more responsive to the plight of their marginal populations, which are becoming larger and more visible. City museums may have a critically important role to play in this arena, even more important than their potential role in city planning, because their primary focus is on the valuation of culture and identity.

Furthermore, city museums may help local populations link to other organizations in other cities. City museums need to be engaged in comparison studies between the home city and other city initiatives. As cities and their populations understand better the experiences of other initiatives, their ability to respond effectively to the tensions of a more heterogeneous environment will grow.

4. Stewarding the Development of New City Museums

As suggested above, a city museum can be a powerful tool for enabling change and development in a city. Many cities are now waking up to this fact, and new city museums are created every year.

Challenges include potential competition from other museums as well as issues of negotiations regarding available space, funding, and staff for the new museum. Great care should be invested in determining the relationship between the museum and the public (both local and tourist), and the balance between past, present, and future focus. As already indicated, the museum may take on a more active role in the city's development if municipal leaders can be brought to understand the potential for development in this regard.

There is a need to elaborate clear guidelines for the development of new city museums. Such guidelines will be less focused on managing collections than on the interface between city museums and the population groups in the city they are mandated to represent.

5. Transforming Older City Museums

The developmental effort of the museum community should also focus on supporting the transformation of older city museums as they prepare themselves to meet the new needs of the cities in which they are found.

This process involves a change in culture and values. Existing city museums struggling with these issues should be encouraged to present their case histories and to interface regularly with sociologists, anthropologists, organization scientists, and others who are concerned with cultural and economic change.

The world is changing, and the old models of institutional functioning must be brought into question. Already it is becoming clear that the nature of the public's interest in cultural areas is shifting. We are moving toward a world that expects cultural experiences to be tailored to an individual's personal interests and needs, and to be delivered, at least in part, directly to that individual. At the same time, the public needs to be challenged—indeed, it craves challenge, and a mix of both physical and virtual forms of engagement. The public will come to installations and exhibitions, but these must be combined with podcasts delivered via Blackberry or iPhone to the individual in his or her home. This requires older institutions to rethink how they operate and understand the new world coming into being. It is no longer a case of "same old same old"—new forms of interaction are multiplying and changing the way business is done.[19]

6. Giving Voice to Local Identities

As indicated earlier, our modern cities are increasingly heterogeneous, and this tendency will persist and grow for decades to come and propagate from larger to smaller cities throughout the world. The city museum needs to embrace such changes—indeed, it may serve as a mediator, a forum for exchange, between different ethnic and cultural groups, and hence contribute to the growing and changing dynamics of the city.

Throughout much of the twentieth century, identity was treated as a "root condition" that determined a person's or a group's activities. It was also understood to be unitary—that is, a person had one defining identity, and this identity was determined by place of birth, family origins, ethnic community, and socioeconomic class. Increasingly, country of origin also factored into the notion of personal identity. In those days, you were a citizen of one and only one country—when you emigrated, you eventually gave up that citizenship to become a citizen of a new country.

Those days are, in large part, past. Today, citizenship can usually be multiple. Indeed, we understand identity as being multiple—we may have many different forms of belonging. Some of these may even be contradictory, but in the twenty-first century, we struggle less to reconcile such contradictions. There are too many of them now to be dealt with in any simple way, and the concept of paradox becomes more and more an everyday concession.

City museums should adapt to these changing ideas concerning identity. Whereas for much of the twentieth century, cities were composed of diverse groups of unitary identities, in today's world cities are composed of overlapping groups with multiple identities.

When our identity was understood to be unitary, identity was often associated with sources of pain as well as of joy. Cities were often unkind to groups of a particular identity; these sources of distress remained long in the memory of such groups, and often these were also repressed or neglected in the memory of other groups within the city. In a world where identity has multiplied, such sources of distress may—indeed, must—be dealt with differently. They are important, but it is easier to recognize their presence than it was earlier, although there is also a greater danger of "glossing over them" in the mix of issues that are in play.

City museums may play an important role in highlighting old sores. In addition, they may encourage discussion and exchange around the different needs of different identities within the modern city. There are still areas where groups are neglected in today's cities—the difficulties encountered by persons with disability are symptomatic of the persistence of such problems. Given the increased presence of persons with disability within our modern cities, this is an area that requires attention. How can city museums act to engage not only their multiple ethnic cultures but also different levels of "ableness" as these are enacted within the city's landscape? This is not merely a question of rendering spaces more accessible to the so-called handicapped—rather, this requires a recognition that "ableness" is a continuum within the whole population, and that different forms of "ableness" lead to different groups with distinct identity. The interplay of these different identities within the broader sociocultural and economic fabric is a key component to the twenty-first-century city, and one that city museums must recognize and portray.

Finally, another element in the formation of our now complex and multiple identities is the life of children. Our understanding of children is beginning to change and will continue to evolve over the coming decades. Throughout much of the twentieth century, children have been treated as a "race apart," a special group with an almost magical personality. Toward the end of the century, however, it has become increasingly apparent that, although there are special aspects to our lives as children, children are not as different from our adult selves as we have allowed ourselves to believe. Part of this shift in understanding arises from the changes in our conception of our adult selves—for example, we recognize today that our conscious selves represent only a tiny fraction of what it is to be human. Hence children, who have often been viewed as "less conscious" than adults, are actually just like adults in this way. As we become more aware of how our multiple identities intersect and interact, we will increasingly find that children already experience this in how they grow and develop. Museums have long been focused on providing experiences that attract children and families. This, like the issue of ableness, goes beyond questions of access, however. Instead, the mix of content addressed and the forms by which content is treated need to change, to become more complex and multilayered, and more sensitive to changing perceptions of what it is to be human in today's world.

If museums in general are concerned with memory and the transmission of cultural memory from one generation to the next, it may be argued that city museums are more concerned with identity than with memory, and with the actualization of identity in the changing present, informed by the past and oriented toward the future. To explore the shift in focus from memory to identity, city museums need to engage with researchers in a variety of fields—geographers, sociologists, psychologists, historians, health professionals, and so forth.

7. Exposing City Vulnerabilities

Our cities are likewise vulnerable in a variety of ways to major events. These may arise from external sociopolitical contexts, from the natural environment, or from the internal dynamics of the city's operation. Usually, a city becomes vulnerable when faced with a combination of these—that is, when faced with a natural event that dovetails with a weakness in its internal dynamics.

The case of Hurricane Katrina and New Orleans provides an obvious example, although New York City's vulnerability to air attack on 9/11 may be viewed as providing another. It would be difficult to mount a similar attack by air on the city of Paris, for example—by city law, there are few buildings above eight stories high in central Paris. (Of course, Paris has other vulnerabilities, evidenced by the success of bombings of its underground trains.) However, the New Orleans disaster was precipitated by a large storm combined with a weakly organized municipal infrastructure and the presence of a poor and particularly vulnerable population. The need for more caring cities is nowhere more dramatized than in the example of New Orleans.

The proliferation of extreme "natural" events that result from climate change exacerbates the vulnerabilities of many cities, even those that have very little history of catastrophic events. Likewise, the increasing focus of cities on sustainability resituates the city's development and its susceptibility to be impacted by internal events. Here again there is a need to open up the community to researchers in diverse domains—climatology, resource management, and so on, but also security management professions and disciplines, policing, and coordination. Dealing with internal population vulnerabilities includes addressing issues of disability and movement in an aging population, and hence requires substantial engagement of the health professions, especially public health and rehabilitation science.

8. Supporting City Museums for Small Cities

Although much public attention is focused on the development of so-called global cities (very large megacities), the majority of city museums will be located within smaller cities with smaller budgets. This needs to be recognized, and the distinct issues related to such smaller cities and towns identified and discussed, as has been signaled by Max Hebditch in chapter 9.

This is especially important as the economy shifts away from a nation-state focus, which favored the development of megacities, to a more city-based approach. How will this change in socioeconomic organization affect the development of small cities in today's world? To what extent do small cities also experience a multiplication and mixing of identities, and what is the impact of this on small cities? Likewise, the Internet as a flattener may result in enabling smaller cities to play a larger role in the emerging global economy. Understanding the opportunities the Internet presents for smaller cities is also a key issue.

Partnerships with businesses and community groups are becoming more important for city museums in smaller cities. Indeed, smaller cities may be expected to specialize into areas of strength to be competitive in the global marketplace, and city museums may play a role in promoting and understanding such areas of specialization. The clash of cultures may be less pronounced than in larger cities, but a sensitivity to cultural diversity is important even for smaller cities.

9. Networking Cities and City Museums

As hinted earlier, cities form a network, and city museums need to be sensitive to the organic nature of this emerging space—it is, indeed, more than the sum of its parts. As cities reemerge in the economic landscape of the twenty-first century, it becomes important to understand how their particular economic and environmental context has affected their development and affects their status today, and what insights can be derived from understanding this relationship in other cities. In the peripheral world, sharing information and experience has become one of the major enablers of growth and change. Today, we can benefit from the combined expertise and experience of others in addressing our own development. Indeed, it is becoming evident that cities, regardless of their cultural and geographic location, share more similarities with each other than they do differences. How one city deals with a complex issue may have significant transfer potential for another city. The sharing between city museums of their local context with other cities and city museums can therefore provide an important contribution to the development of the city.

This requires careful thought. What kinds of joint activities should be promoted? How much should city museums engage in online exchanges with other museums and groups around the world? What kinds of shared initiatives could be developed to promote such exchanges?

The issue is not just one of encouraging exchange and developing shared projects, however. City museums need to work through consolidating and vision-generating agencies such as CAMOC to develop a coherent, global program for change and growth. They may need to use virtual tools, such as described in section 10 below, to coordinate and experiment collectively with new ideas. Today, although a certain amount of such experimentation is going on, it is often limited to a few far-seeing museums. One of the lessons the Internet has taught is that collective actions, when organized in an appropriate manner, may lead to new forms of understanding that cannot be accessed individually. City museums need to find ways of developing collective programs to function effectively in the emerging world.

10. Integrating Cities, City Museums, and Virtual Environments

In very general terms, the Internet provides a new environment for museums to communicate with the public. For city museums, the Internet constitutes potentially a highly enabling medium for activating their relationship with the public, at the local and regional levels but also nationally and internationally. Blogs have become a primary means for engaging the public, and city museums could and should take advantage of the opportunities this tool provides.

Wikipedia also provide a powerful tool for representing knowledge—indeed, wikis are emerging as the primary knowledge repository for the world's populations. Although some concerns have been raised about the reliability of wikis, they have become key elements of our knowledge about the world. Museums should be at the forefront of developing appropriate wiki content— they are de facto knowledge repositories. Museums at the very least should be present in the world of wikis. In the long term, some museums may actually become a part of the wiki network—the potential is certainly there.

In addition to blogs, wikis, and websites, however, the advent of virtual worlds such as Second Life heralds a new era for the unification of the world. Second Life is a three-dimensional simulacrum of the world, with its own geography,[20] economy,[21] and cultural life. It has broken the barrier of ten million users and is still doubling every few months; a year from now, if this rate of growth continues—and it has remained steady for more than four years—it will have one hundred million users. Already virtual museums abound within Second Life, including art museums, natural history museums, and science museums.[22] Hundreds of art galleries are to be found in Second Life, and new ones are emerging all the time. As for city museums, a variety of cities (Amsterdam, Berlin, Tokyo, Florence, Paris, etc.) are in the process of developing digital versions of themselves on Second Life, and these constitute a form of virtual city museum.

Many people believe that virtual worlds will replace the Internet of today—they offer access to today's websites and information sources, but in addition, access to a whole new world of experiences. And they are not much harder to learn than was the World Wide Web to begin with. Although today Second Life is leading the way, there are several new virtual worlds on the horizon that will create competition for Linden Labs, the host of Second Life.

Virtual worlds, because of their social as well as three-dimensional character, offer a superb platform for city museums to explore city spaces as they are today or via historical recreations (for example, the Paris reproduction in Second Life dates from 1900, and there is a reproduction of ancient Rome as well). Indeed, the real interest of virtual worlds is how they can become integrated into our everyday lives. Ultimately, it is possible for city museums to become implicated into the daily lives of a city's inhabitants or its visitors, whether these are real or virtual.

Not all museums have been successful at using the Internet to gain better access to the public. This issue needs to be examined more carefully and critically. Success stories need to be brought forward, but also, perhaps even especially, the failures. Why have some efforts to develop a viable virtual audience for city museums failed? The issue of virtual worlds also requires new development and new initiatives. An online forum for these issues might make good sense, and it fits within the virtual environment.

CONCLUSION

City museums today are to be found at the fulcrum of a whole new set of roles and behaviors than were available to them in the past. Within our rapidly changing world, characterized by a process of peripheralization of its economy and social structures and a flattening of its communication structures, cities are emerging as the workhorses of the new economy. As a result, city museums are poised to play, not a "central" role, but a critically important one. This point is important. City museums, often housed centrally in massive buildings, may need to reexamine their assumption or desire to become more central. The world that is coming into being favors, on the contrary, structures and organizations that are more horizontal, peripheral, more collaborative, and distributed. However, regardless of the organizational structure adopted by the modern city museum, its vocation is likely to become more important, not less, as society enters a new era.

These are exciting times for city museums, but they are also challenging times. There is a need to recognize the mix of changes in play, but also to devote resources to improving our understanding of the roles city museums may take up within new urban arrangements. Research and visioning activities are therefore more important than ever. Indeed, while museums traditionally function one step behind the evolving world, city museums today are poised to be one step ahead!

NOTES

This work was financially supported via the Canada Research Chair in Cognitive Geomatics.

1. U.S. Census Bureau, 1998, www.census.gov/ipc/prod/wp98/ib98-4.pdf; Janet Larsen, "Population Growing by 80 Million Annually," 2002, www.earth-policy .org/Indicators/indicator1.htm; United Nations Department of Economic and Social Affairs, Population Division, *World Urbanization Prospects: The 2000 Revision* (New York: United Nations Publications, 2001), www.un.org/spanish/esa/population/wpp2000h.pdf.

2. J. L. Simon links economic growth to population size; see *Theory of Population and Economic Growth* (Oxford: Blackwell, 1986). The Rand Corporation presents various scenarios; see "Banking the 'Demographic Dividend': How Population Dynamics Can Affect Economic Growth," RB-5065 (2002), www.rand.org/pubs/research_briefs/RB5065/index1.html.

3. Thomas Bolioli, "Theoretical Framework for a Unified Model of Population and Economic Growth," 2001, risprawl.terranovum.com/other/tbolioli-2001-march.html.

4. For example, see Gyorgy Korniss and Thomas Caraco, "Spatial Dynamics of Invasion: The Geometry of Introduced Species," *Journal of Theoretical Biology* 233, no. 1 (2005): 137–150, arxiv.org/pdf/cond-mat/0501512.

5. Robert Abinzano, "Globalization, Regions, and Borders," UNESCO Management of Social Transformations (MOST) Discussion Paper No. 27, 1999, unesdoc.unesco.org/images/0011/001149/114958eo.pdf.

6. Thomas L. Friedman, *The World Is Flat: A Brief History of the Twenty-First Century,* 2nd ed. (Toronto: Douglas & McIntyre, 2006).

7. Jeffrey D. Sachs, "Can Extreme Poverty Be Eliminated?" *Scientific American* (September 2005).

8. Jane Jacobs, *The Economy of Cities* (New York: Vintage, 1970).

9. Ivo Maroevic, "Museology as a Field of Knowledge," *ICOM Study Series* 8 (2002): 5–7, icom.museum/study_series_pdf/8_ICOM-ICOFOM.pdf.

10. For an example of such work, see Magellan Egoyan (Geoffrey Edwards) et al., embodiedresearch.blogspot.com.

11. Heritage Canada, 2007, www.canadianheritage.gc.ca/progs/multi/canada2017/2_e.cfm.

12. Marco Bontje and Jan Latten, "Stable Size, Changing Composition: Recent Migration Dynamics of the Dutch Large Cities," *Royal Dutch Geographical Society Journal* 96, no. 4 (2005): 444–451, ideas.repec.org/a/bla/tvecsg/v96y2005i4p444-451.html.

13. Statistics Canada, "Prevalence of disability in Canada," 2003, www.statcan.ca/english/freepub/89-577-XIE/canada.htm; see also David Foot, *Boom, Bust and Echo: How to Profit from the Coming Demographic Shift* (Cincinnati, OH: St. Anthony Messenger Press, 1996).

14. Andrew Sum, Ishwar Khatiwada, Paulo Tobar, Sheila Palma, and Joseph McLaughlin, "The Adult Disabled Population (16–74) in Massachusetts: Its Size and Demographic/Socioeconomic Composition in 2003–2004," 2006, www.clms.neu.edu/publication/documents/first_mrc_report_in_2006.pdf.

15. Australian Bureau of Statistics, "Trends and Projections in Disability in Western Australia," 2005, www.disability.wa.gov.au/dscwr/_assets/main/guidelines/documents/doc/trendsfactsheet05_(id_2774_ver_1.0.0).doc.

16. Irving Zola, "Disability Statistics: What We Count and What It Tells Us: A Personal and Political Analysis," *Journal of Disability Policy Studies* 4, no. 2 (1993).

17. United Nations Department of Economic and Social Affairs, *World Urbanization Prospects 2000*.

18. Charles W. Dean, Richard Lumb, Kevin Proctor, James Klopovic, Amy Hyatt, and Rob Hamby, *Social Work and Law Enforcement Partnerships: A Summons to the Village*, 2000, North Carolina Department of Crime Control and Public Safety, www.ncgccd.org/pubs/SWAPP.pdf.

19. Friedman, *The World Is Flat*.

20. mageEgo, 2007, www.youtube.com/watch?v=R-Nbu17gSNM.

21. mageEgo, 2007, www.youtube.com/watch?v=Bt8L2hr-m4I.

22. Richard Urban, Paul Marty, and Michael Twidale, "A Second Life for Your Museum: 3D Multi-User Virtual Environments and Museums, Archives, and Museum Informatics," 2007, *Conference on Museums and the Web 2007*, www.archimuse.com/mw2007/papers/urban/urban.html.

12

From Urban Blocks to City Blogs

Defining Attributes for the City Museum of Today

Marlen Mouliou

SETTING THE AGENDA

This chapter's goal is twofold: to explore the attributes that can currently define the work of city museums and to assess if and how these attributes are adopted by city museums in their quest to become effective and vibrant within the city and the communities they must serve. To fulfill this dual aim, current museum theory and empirical data drawn from research[1] the author conducted in 2006 on the operation of city museums will be brought into play, along with city life experiences and a personal understanding of how the network society can shape our world in general and the museum world in particular. But first, a recent example of social activism will be presented as a preamble to an exploration of the special role that thought and action in civil society can potentially play in museum practice.

At the end of June 2007, extensive fires burned down more than 4,000 hectares of forest in the Parnitha National Park, the last remaining green belt around the city of Athens and a designated Special Protection Area. Many Greeks have been devastated and enraged by the loss of the capital's

largest forest and in the aftermath, fears have arisen about major consequences for the environment. Politicians announced measures to offset the
effect, and various ecological nongovernmental organizations (NGOs) and
experts offered scientific advice on the best ways for reforestation and the
conservation of fauna. However, what has been unprecedented and re-
markable has been the reaction of ordinary people, which took the form of
text messages written on Internet blogs and mobile phones. Just a day or
two after the blaze, a text message was sent by an anonymous blogger to
many others, and then made the rounds, urging people to attend a protest
rally outside Parliament. "Sunday 8 July, 7pm, outside parliament," the
message said. "Demand the reforestation of all burned land. Measures far
from political expediency are required. Don't be inactive this time. Pass this
message on to as many as you can"—and indeed, thousands of citizens
gathered before Parliament on July 8 to protest over the Parnitha catastro-
phe. It was very clear that many people were willing to act on their emotions and take a proactive stance toward the fate and future of the city they
live in. "The reforestation of Parnitha concerns us all, and we need to bat-
tle it with our own hands and the internet," stated a blogger.[2] Over the
course of the next few days, a host of other events and demonstrations demanding action were circulated by e-mail.

Blogs, this people-centered network of social media and the modern
version of personal diaries, managed to mobilize instantly the people of
Athens and make their voices heard. Could or should a city museum possibly manage to take a similarly activist role in the protection of the quality of life in the city it represents?

ICONS OF URBAN IDENTITY, MIRRORS
OF CITY LIFE, PLATFORMS FOR CIVIL ACTION

Museums shape cities and are themselves shaped by cities in many different ways. For some scholars, museums act as classical icons[3] for urban centrality and identity and as instruments of the urban growth machine.[4] City
museums more specifically are perceived as places "where civic, social and
industrial urban history is collected and presented."[5] However, as narrators
of the story of urban development, they often have to do more with bricks

than with people and may get disconnected from the city that is around them. Often, city museums, "while they have so much to say about the past, have little to say about our present urban condition, and even less about our possible futures."[6]

Over the last ten to fifteen years, a great deal of effort has been put into enhancing the connection between museums and urban communities, and today, innovative (and successful) museum practice is becoming much more common.[7] Increasingly, the task of a museum is to deal not only with the past of the city, but its present and future as well, in order to contribute actively to the city's development and help reinforce a sense of place and identity. Museums can, and frequently do, "act as a starting-point for the discovery of the city, which can lead people to look with fresh, more informed and tolerant eyes at the richness of the present urban environment and to imagine beyond it to past and possible future histories."[8] This statement by Nichola Johnson is quoted elsewhere in this book, a testament to its encapsulation of the aims of the contemporary museum of the city.

Some of the most characteristic functions of museums of cities could be summarized as follows:

- Museums can give a sense of order to urban chaos.
- They can act as hallmarks of urban identity and traditions.
- They are vehicles for urban regeneration or at least they can help halt urban deterioration.
- They can be symbols of an urban historic heritage.
- They can be meeting grounds for socially different groups. Depending on their mission and their policies, they can reinforce social segregation or act as agents of social inclusion and rapprochement between the rich and the poor of a city.

Today, in the information age, there have been many radical changes in communication, socialization, knowledge, and lifelong learning. Blogs, for instance, have features and qualities that can be very interesting in any exploration of how a city museum can work within its urban context. The emergence of the Internet and blogging[9] has undoubtedly brought a revolution. Blogs function as personal online diaries. They provide commentary or news, not only as partisan gossipers, but also as fast sensors of changes and as disseminators of key information in the public domain. They take the form of user-generated content and open-source journalism, allowing readers to leave comments and other material in an interactive format. They take a nonauthoritative tone and are more democratic, open to debate, independent, and wide ranging. They give readers new perspectives on various topics and offer different viewpoints from those of official news sources; thus they can potentially shape public views and attitudes. They combine text, images, and other media, and link to other blogs. They can be accessed potentially by vast numbers of Internet users and in practice are very popular among young people. They become tools for outreach and opinion forming, shining light on places and people other media often ignore. They are inclusive and encourage contacts among many different lifestyles. They are activist in nature and dare break the status quo. They seek constant reapproval, as their popularity is frequently monitored and assessed, for their editorials and opinions are voted on. They can be a tool for in-depth analysis of any topic by experts. They are an inexpensive medium, affordable by people of low income. They are omnipresent, once you log in.

These features do not characterize exclusively the blogger's network paradigm, but also other popular communication and information media such as the free press, which circulate either in the form of daily newspaper or weekly publications, covering more specialized fields such as culture and life in the city today. *Athens Voice*[10] and *Lifo*,[11] for instance, two magazines that comment on life in the Greek capital, give a sense of what is happening in the city; reflect on the cognitive, affective, and emotional stimuli of the urban environment; and create subjective mental maps and urban visions for their readers. Both online and in a printed format, they have become reference points in the city's weekly cycle, by gaining general approval and a large readership; remarkably, they reach out successfully to social groups that are more complex in their needs and expectations, such as teenagers and young adults. These free-press city magazines can be found literally everywhere in Athens: in the streets, metro and bus stations, bookshops, snack bars, restaurants, museums, and other points of distribution. They also provide membership and a site for Athens bloggers. Very creative in their graphic design, with varied topics and a contemporary, youthful style of journalism based on a user-generated content philosophy, which allows all their subscribers to upload comments, texts, images, and so forth, they offer a free, good-quality cultural communication within and about the city. They offer a service to the city whose weekly pulse is transmitted in a lively way through their pages, paper or electronic.

But what does the blog and free-press philosophy and practice have to do with museums, and what do we attempt to argue here? Is it that a city museum today must have its own blog or free-press publication in order to be more successful in reaching out to its public and building up new audiences? The answer could be a positive one, but our intention goes beyond this simple association. Rather, the objective is to focus on the generic elements and qualities of a successful blog or free-press product (see table 12.1) that can inspire city museums to offer a better service to cities and their people.

DEFINING ATTRIBUTES FOR THE TWENTY-FIRST-CENTURY CITY MUSEUM

Some of these qualities are not unknown territory for many museums today. Museums have traditionally been collecting institutions, smaller or larger repositories of material artifacts of the past. But the "concept of museums responding to audiences as partners in a joint enterprise"[12] has been

Table 12.1. Generic Qualities of Quality Blogs and Free Press

Open-sourced, multi-vocal, collaborative, involving, promoters of dialogue and debate
Informative and constantly updated, intellectually intelligent
Humane, people-centered, emotionally intelligent
Seekers of innovation and constructive reformation
Users of honest, clear, and assertive language
Multimedia, dynamic-looking
Relevant for the present and forward-looking
Critical of the self and the others
Omnipresent in time and space
Freely accessed by all

ranking high in the agenda of museum professionals for more than fifteen years. Museums around the world have been increasingly reviewing their institutional, educational, and social role, and assessing their impact on people's lives. More and more they aim to tell interesting stories about the past, the present, and the future in a challenging and compelling way. Current thinking on the role of city museums, as well as current practice, is along these lines. City museums are centers of knowledge and inspiring learning; recipients of objects and stories reflecting the past and contemporary life of the various communities in the city; formulators of cultural identity and informed citizenship in a globalized world; agents for social inclusion, cultural understanding, and tolerance; professional institutions in the public realm with the responsibility of being accountable to their users and nonusers, as well as to the governmental and nongovernmental bodies that guide and accredit their work.

Table 12.2. Generic Features of Twenty-First-Century Museums

The reinvented museum	*The engaging museum*
Shared vision and goals; multiple viewpoints	An object treasure-house significant to all local communities
Shared leadership and decision making—bottom-up management	Involving the community in product development and delivery
Mission-driven; mission-related activities	An agent for physical, economic, cultural, and social regeneration, with a core purpose of improving people's lives
Equitable, inclusive, multicultural; external focus; broad representation; open in communication and welcoming differences and dialogue	Accessible to all, in every way—a celebrant of cultural diversity and a promoter of social cohesion
Social responsibility; informed risk taker; strategically positioned; proactive	Proactive in supporting neighborhood and community renewal
Relevant and forward-looking	Relevant to the whole of society
Audience-focused and responsive; community-based; exchanging knowledge	Proactive in developing new audiences; integral to the learning community
Knowledgeable about audiences; earned value; public accountability; institutional assessment	An exemplar of quality service provision
Entrepreneurial	An income generator

Based on the models of the so-called reinvented[13] or engaging[14] new museum, we can summarize this new institutional vision in table 12.2. It cannot be easily estimated how many city museums have already adopted these new attributes and to what extent and level of commitment. In 2006, during a two-month survey conducted on behalf of Volos Municipal Center for Historical Research and Documentation, the author tried to gather and analyze data that would shed light on a handful of core questions:

- What is the current institutional, financial, conceptual, and social framework of the operation of city museums around the world?
- What are their present visions, missions, and aims, and how do they fulfill them?
- What sort of stories about the cities and their communities do they choose to narrate, and what types of media do they tend to use to interpret city life in the past and present?
- What is the level of their social involvement and commitment toward establishing meaningful and creative dialogue and partnerships with their local communities?
- How do they assess their own strengths and weaknesses, and how do they perceive the opportunities and threats that arise and may determine their current and future work?
- Can we trace different trends, ideas, and practices that are geographically and culturally related, and if so, how can we explain them?
- Are there examples of best practice within the city museums sector, and what are the pathways they open up for other city museums?

This questionnaire-based survey was addressed to more than 150 city museums around the world in order to gather quantitative and qualitative data that would potentially help the author plot patterns of operation, identify and analyze both well-known and less-well-known examples of best practice, and generally get a better picture of the functioning of city museums internationally. Eventually, thirty-five city[15] museums responded, representing eighteen European and five non-European countries. The great majority of them have been recently redeveloped (80 percent); are housed in historical, often iconic, listed (protected by the state or region, as buildings of outstanding merit) city landmarks[16] (77 percent); and rely significantly on public funding[17] for their operation (83 percent). These museums are mostly run by local authorities (69 percent), more than half of them (57 percent) operate under recently amended constitutions, and almost[18] all of them (a striking 92 percent) have collections that belong to them. Although the sample is not very large, it is nevertheless fairly representative, for Europe at least, and certainly provides ample information for analysis and the drawing of conclusions. Here we shall focus on some key findings and observations regarding museum policy making; the scope and use of museum collections; exhibition modes and interpretative media; matters of learning, access, and social commitment; and current stances on best practice as well as future perspectives.

To start with policy making: Collecting and access policies are important for more than half of the museums (66 percent and 60 percent accordingly), but learning and display policies are much less so (37 percent, 29 percent). In fact, all museums that stated they have implemented learning and display policies have been examples from the United Kingdom;[19] this finding reflects recent strategic actions taken in this country for encouraging inspirational learning and accessibility for all. Two-thirds of the museums (69 percent) undertake systematic contemporary collecting, often under the umbrella of specific collecting policies. What to collect in order to reflect contemporary life in the city is certainly a hard decision and requires an organized plan. For these thirty-five museums, the most common selection criteria for contemporary collecting are the objects' relevance to city history (50 percent), their role in documenting city changes and everyday life[20] (33 percent), their provenance (29 percent), and their conformity with specific collecting policies (25 percent).

Oral history—the history of ordinary people—enables us to learn about the past through the firsthand accounts of those who actually experienced it. It offers new knowledge by challenging accepted judgments and by cross-referencing plural alternative voices. Thus it can lead to new attitudes and values by the immediacy of emotions and feelings it conveys. More than half of the museums in this sample (60 percent) systematically collect oral history testimonies. Academic or curatorial considerations are the most common reason for doing so (76 percent). Oral history's great potential as an interpretation medium that contextualizes and personalizes objects (71 percent) and as an asset for community work (57 percent) is also greatly recognized. Museums that collect oral history tend to be more self-aware of their important educational and social role, the challenges for more openness to society and to partnerships with citizens.[21]

As one would expect, the most common interpretive media used by the museums are "authentic objects" (91 percent) and "display panels" (80 percent), whereas only one-third of them use "living memory displays" (37 percent), "storytelling" (34 percent), "role play" (31 percent), and "discovery activities" (31 percent), which offer alternative, less authoritative, and open-ended modes of interpretation. In the new Museum of Liverpool, however, a shift in the approach to displaying objects and conveying information will be taken by employing a uniquely flexible exhibition system. This decision is grounded on the understanding that history is continuously being written, while the people, the city, and the region hold many different stories that must be told. Museums, therefore, have to transform and adapt quickly and efficiently as living parts of the community; they must be dynamic and forward looking.

Local communities and school groups are the predominant target audiences of the museums in this sample. Most of them thus prefer to focus on themes and topics such as "local events" (91 percent), "home life" (77 percent), "personal stories" (77 percent), the "natural and built environment" (74 percent), "work" (71 percent), "arts and crafts" (69 percent). Difficult or controversial subject matter is not often at the top of their preferences, perhaps because it is not really easy to talk about issues that are in the center of contemporary social debate (such as cultural diversity, poverty, social exclusion, etc.). So "popular health" (37 percent), "religion and morality" (37 percent), "hygiene" (37 percent), "crime and law" (31 percent) rate much lower.

An impressive number of museums (77 percent of the total sample) say they develop specific strategies to attract nonusers, 69 percent implement audience and evaluation work, 65 percent have an interest in developing projects that will empower socially excluded individuals or communities, and 86 percent develop links and work with local community groups. Their aim to build up audiences and create stronger links with individuals or communities at risk of exclusion is realized in many different ways—for example, projects to set up community exhibitions together,[22] cross-cultural policy and strategic actions,[23] outreach work[24] that assists people to present aspects of their life to a wider audience and give them more confidence to effect changes in their own situation, marketing,[25] admission policies,[26] the Web,[27] special workshops,[28] and so on. The list cannot be exhaustive.

The city museum sector is well aware of the many new challenges that have to be faced now and in the coming years. City museums are not always certain about the current predominant features that define their profile, but one-third of them (31 percent) believe they are "community oriented" and those that say so do actually develop strategies to attract nonusers, to help people at risk, and to create links with the community. On the other hand, 29 percent say they are more "research-based"; a striking 80 percent believe they are "multifaceted." However, rather less than half of the museums (only 40 percent to 45 percent) could say that their exhibitions are "people-oriented," "emotive" experiences. Is this because many museums are still apprehensive of acting as informed risk takers? Is it that they prefer to be the voice of authority and focus on the past rather than offer multiple viewpoints that are relevant for their communities today?

"Committed community of museum professionals" and "new funding opportunities" (69 percent, 66 percent) are considered by many museums as driving forces for institutional changes that would make their operation more dynamic and effective. Only 14 percent regard self-critical "performance assessment" as important, a fact that may be seen as a hesitation on the part of museum professionals to accept the purpose and value of self-accountability. Accordingly, the "lack of funding" is by far (74 percent) the major restraining force that inhibits museums, mainly in central and eastern Europe, to go ahead with development projects and changes that would have an effect on their future profile. This restraining force is less important for museums in western Europe, where more dynamic strategies to raise revenue have been followed in recent years. "Limited partnerships

FIGURE 12.1
Culturally diverse audiences visiting the "London before London" gallery at the Museum of London. © Museum of London.

with local communities" (51 percent) are also considered a major restraining force for the growth and expansion of city museum work.

The survey questionnaire sought also to assess, based on six predetermined statements, the stance of museums toward inspirational learning, the communities' self-representation in the museum, and the museum's role as a forum of civic dialogue (see appendix, part 5, 5a–f). The museums were asked to evaluate the importance of these statements for their own current and future work. Based on the ratings provided, we can suggest that museums operating in northern, western, and eastern Europe as well as those beyond the continent are keener to endorse the core values of these statements. This is much less apparent in museums located in central and southern Europe. The majority of museums,[29] however, disagree with the statement "Self-representation by communities is a priority in our museum," a finding which may indicate that city museums are still rather cautious or negative toward "a user generating content" philosophy and practice. Museums that carry out audience research tend to agree more with the values of these statements, but the difference between those that do carry out audience research and those that don't is not as statistically significant as one might expect.

Self-assessment, the exercise of measuring one's strengths against one's weaknesses, is always useful for individuals and institutions alike. The data gathered in this survey by means of two pertinent open-ended questions reveal that city museums have qualities and weak points that touch both upon their traditional and reinvented institutional identities. The fact that museums hold collections outstanding in quality, size, and thematic breadth is perceived by many city museums as their principal strength. Community-oriented institutional missions and the presence of dedicated and expert staff also rate high in their self-assessment opinions. This finding is indicative of the new people-centered nature and purpose of many more city museums. On the other hand, the shortage of financial resources along with the absence of effective fund-raising work and the lack of adequate and appropriate infrastructure are picked out as key weaknesses. Interestingly, museums also recognize that if they want to develop further and grow, they must invest more in carrying out systematic and frequent audience research. Some key comments on museum strengths and weaknesses are presented in epigrammatic format in table 12.3.

City museums, no matter how long or short their history is, can always look within the sector to get ideas and inspiration for further improving their practices. The exemplary inspirational institutions[30] do not always strictly fall into the city museum category, but the reasons they give for voting for one or another are certainly informative, as we can assess by looking at the data presented in table 12.4. The association of these benchmarking choices with the generic qualities of blogs and a free press, as defined earlier in this paper, can also be enlightening. One can easily notice that most of the reasons in the lefthand column of the table, relating to views on best museum practice, find their parallel in the qualities shown in the righthand column of the table, which define the profile of quality blogs.

By way of conclusion, we can recall what urban specialists[31] pinpoint regarding the urban phenomenon. Today, there are a good twenty megacities (cities with more than ten million inhabitants) and a vast number of city

Table 12.3. Key Strengths and Weaknesses of City Museums

Strengths	Frequency	Weaknesses	Frequency
Material resources (collections, buildings, infrastructure)			
Superb collections (in quality and size)	17	Lack of money and inadequacy of fund-raising work	12
Accessible building in the city center	3	Inadequate infrastructure—need for expansion	9
Attractive historical building	3	Maintenance problems—restoration	5
Good infrastructure	2	Lack of storage space	3
Fully accessible collections	1	Limited physical access	3
Museum spread in many locations	1	Building not easy to find	3
Object loans come from the community	1	Need for more accessible collections / digitization and outreach programs	3
Good fund-raising schemes	1		
Human resources (leader, staff, partnerships)			
Dedicated and expert staff	8	Understaffed—lack of experts	6
Effective partnerships with local authority and other heritage managers	7		
Inspiring leader	1		
Flexible	1		
Eager volunteers	1		
Mission, aims, roles			
Community-oriented	10	Need for more audience research	9
Reputable among the local community—distinctive brand	8	More interdisciplinary research	1
Interested in children and young people	3	Work more on its profile, locally and globally	1
International orientation	2	Lack of support from local authorities	1
Distinguished research	2	Weak business-base	1
Lots of good ideas	1	Need to attract younger audiences	2
Learning and interpretation			
Interesting subject matter	5	Need for redisplay	2
Many and lively temporary exhibitions	5	More marketing	2
Good educational programs	4	Weak events program	2
Intimate, speaks to feelings	2	Need for new media displays	2
Wide provision of services	2	Need for more programs targeting school groups	1
Good design	2		
Intimate and unconventional	1		
Confrontational but safe	1		
Interdisciplinary	1		

Source: Survey data

**Table 12.4. Benchmarking in the City Museum Sector:
Key Reasons for Selecting Museums of Best Practice**

Reasons for selecting benchmarking city museums	Frequency	Generic qualities of blogs and free press
Superb collections	9	
Good outreach and community programs	8	Open-sourced, multi-vocal, collaborative and involving, promoters of dialogue and debate
Interesting changing exhibitions	7	Informative and constantly updated, intellectually intelligent
Dynamic exhibition policy	7	Multimedia, dynamic-looking
Dynamic presence in the city in the overall	4	Omnipresent in time and space
Innovative	3	Seekers of innovation and constructive reform
Empowering and friendly	3	Humane, people-centered, emotionally intelligent
High potential	2	Relevant for the present and forward-looking
Committed museum professionals	2	Critical of the self and others
Open-minded local authority	2	Relevant to the present and forward-looking
Museographical excellence	2	Multimedia, dynamic-looking
Good digital resources (guides, animations)	2	Multimedia, dynamic-looking
Fascinating life stories of the people and the city	2	Humane, people-centered, emotionally intelligent
Exceptional numbers of visitors and well-embedded in the local communities	2	Accessed by all
Chosen topics	2	Informative and constantly updated, intellectually intelligent
Good organizational structure	2	
Hands-on exhibits / interactive displays	1	Multimedia, dynamic-looking
Good storage space	1	
Good publications	1	
Accessible collections	1	
Multi-location museum	1	Omnipresent in time and space
Fund-raising capacity	1	

Source: Survey data

regions with over one million inhabitants. Each city, of course, has different characteristics as well as varying levels of success in managing urban change. Cities expand upward and outward—they never stand still—and indeed it is a very challenging task for any city museum to capture these rapid changes and interpret them in meaningful ways, both personally and collectively. It is our belief that a city museum has to be a fast runner, an honest and sharp-sighted observer of city life and its people, an activist seeker of its many faces. In this quest, it may be useful to adopt some, if not all of the generic elements that are to be found in quality blogs. And if museum mission statements[32] tell the truth, then there are quite a few museums in the sample of this survey research that use compelling words to describe their vision and commitment toward their city and its people.

APPENDIX—STRUCTURE OF THE SURVEY QUESTIONNAIRE

Various museum and organizational theories, international museum policy guidelines, and a number of research reports that create the framework for an ongoing discussion on the features of the traditional versus the reinvented museum, formed the baseline for this survey research. The structure of the five-part survey questionnaire with its numerous subthemes follows.

Parts 1 and 2: Museum Details and Management

1. Date of museum foundation
2. Date of the most recent major redevelopment of the museum
3. Institutional profile and governance
4. Brand name and its popularity
5. Type of museum building and available facilities
6. Financial operation and viability
7. Mission statements, aims, and date of constitutional amendments
8. Museum policy making

Part 3: Museum Collections and Research

1. Diversity of collections
2. Ownership of collections
3. Contemporary collecting and defined criteria for this type of collecting

4. Subject areas covered by museum narratives
5. Use of oral history in the museum, purposes and scope

Part 4: Museum Interpretation, Learning, Access, and Social Commitment
1. Exhibition modes and conceptual frameworks
2. Exhibition experiences offered
3. Information resources offered for the collections, on display and in store
4. Interpretive media used in the exhibitions (and the extent of their use)
5. Types of learning provision offered to meet the needs of diverse audiences
6. Museum audiences
   a. Actual visitor numbers
   b. Main target groups
   c. Development and types of strategies to attract nonusers
   d. Employment of oral history and outreach officers
   e. Audience research, methodologies used and their frequency
   f. Evaluation of museum accessibility (physical, intellectual, social)
   g. Strategies to empower socially excluded (or at risk of exclusion) individuals and communities
   h. Development of links with local community groups and kinds of partnerships with them

Part 5: Overall Assessment of Institutional Stances, Perspectives, and Benchmark Work
1. Museum self-appraisal regarding its core priorities and institutional profile
2. Museum strengths and weaknesses
3. Driving and restraining forces for the operation of the museum toward a more challenging future
4. Examples of best practices that operate as models of operation for city museums
5. Museum stances toward the issues of inspirational learning, the self-representation of communities in the museum, the museum's role as a forum of civic dialogue, and exploration of contemporary urban issues

a. Inspirational learning is paramount. The museum must encourage everyone to experience, think, question, enjoy, understand, and challenge.

b. The museum has an obligation to provide multiple means of exploring and responding to objects and ideas, for there are many different kinds of learners and learning styles.

c. Self-representation by communities is a priority in our museum.

d. A city museum must help its audiences understand why the city they know is the way it is.

e. A city museum must be a forum for debate, where different perspectives can be explored and critical thinking developed.

f. A city museum must find out what the local community needs and adjust its work accordingly.

NOTES

1. In December 2005, Volos Municipal Center for Historical Research and Documentation invited the author to contribute to the process of idea gathering and principle formation that would eventually define the character, identity, mission, policies, and agenda of Volos city museum. The author's proposal was first to look more systematically at the most recent development in the field of city museum theory and practice, as well as draw from the current museological literature on broader core issues such as access, learning, interpretation, and social engagement in museums. Secondly, the proposal provided for the designing and implementation of survey research that would empirically trace and map stances, best practices, and trends that currently existed in the city museum sector around the world. The research tool chosen for this project was a lengthy questionnaire, consisting of close-ended, semi-open, and open-ended questions, as a way to provide an array of useful insights for quantitative and qualitative analysis. The data gathered could thus define paths for strategic action for the Volos museum project team and its developing work. At a second level, they could also be a useful source of information and an advocacy tool for city museums in general. This research has been published in Greek, both as a detailed internal report and as a shorter feature article in *En Volo*, a quality magazine published by the Municipality of Volos. See Marlen Mouliou, "Mapping

the 'World' of City Museums: Traces and Clues," *En Volo* 22 (July–September 2006): 8–17.

2. Many blogs have been actively promoting dissemination of information on this matter. One of them is called *anadasosi* (reforestation) and can be reached at anadasosi.blogspot.com.

3. See chapter 2 by Georges Prévélakis, "City Museums and the Geopolitics of Globalization."

4. For the role of museums in urban regeneration, see for instance Pedro Lorente, ed., *The Role of Museums and the Arts in the Urban Regeneration of Liverpool* (Leicester: Center for Urban History, University of Leicester, 1996), and Volker Kirchberg, "Categorizing Urban Tasks: Functions of Museums in the Post-Industrial City," *Curator* 46, no. 1 (2003): 60–79.

5. Kirchberg, "Categorizing Urban Tasks," 61.

6. Ian Jones, "A City Museum for the Twenty-First Century: Cardiff's Example," *En Volo* 22 (July–September 2006): 25 (in Greek).

7. There is a growing body of important literature on city museum theory and practice. For some ground reading on this topic, see Gaynor Kavanagh and Elizabeth Frostick, eds., *Making City Histories in Museums* (Leicester: Leicester University Press, 1998); Renée Kistemaker, ed., *City Museums as Centers of Civic Dialogue? Proceedings of the Fourth Conference of the International Association of City Museums, Amsterdam, 3–5 November 2005* (Amsterdam Historical Museum, 2006); issues 187 and 231 of *Museum International,* titled *City Museums* (1995) and *Urban Life and Museums* (2006); Robert R. Archibald, *The New Town Square: Museums and Communities in Transition* (Walnut Creek, CA: AltaMira Press, 2004); Nick Merriman, "The Peopling of London Project," in *Cultural Diversity: Redeveloping Museum Audiences in Britain,* ed. Eilean Hooper-Greenhill (Leicester: Leicester University Press, 1997), 119–148; Simon Stephens, "City Limits," *Museums Journal* 105, no. 10 (October 2005): 22–25; for international and Greek city museum practice, see special issue of *En Volo,* "City Museum in the Twenty-First Century," *En Volo* 22 (July–September 2006) (in Greek).

8. Nichola Johnson, "Discovering the City," *Museum International,* no. 187, vol. 47, no. 3 (July–September 1995): 6.

9. In May 2007, the blog search engine Technorati was tracking more than 71 million blogs, peaking up now to 100 million. In Greece there are currently at least 7,500 blogs commenting on many topics, many of which relate to city life and experiences. Blogging has also brought a range of legal liabilities and other often unforeseen consequences especially in politically sensitive areas, but here we would like to focus on the positive aspects of blogging, which can be a source of inspiration for the work and operation of city museums.

10. Available also online in www.athensvoice.gr.

11. Available also online in www.lifo.gr.

12. Graham Black, *The Engaging Museum: Developing Museums for Visitor Involvement* (London: Routledge, 2005): 3.

13. David Anderson, *Reinventing the Museum* (Walnut Creek, CA: Rowman & Littlefield, 2004): 2, table 1.

14. Black, *The Engaging Museum*, 4, box 0.1.

15. Since there is no existing corpus of museums about cities, the selection of the sample was based on (a) knowledge of relevant examples drawn from the author's personal knowledge; (b) the museological literature; (c) the international scientific forums and previous conferences on the subject of city museums; (d) the work of CAMOC, the International Council of Museums (ICOM) international committee for museums of cities; (e) extensive search on various museum databases on the Internet; (f) previous reports on closely related topics such as the reports in Sandra Parker et al., *Neighborhood Renewal and Social Inclusion: The Role of Museums, Archives and Libraries* (London: Resource and University of Northumbria, 2002); Eilean Hooper-Greenhill et al., *Museums and Social Inclusion: The GLLAM Report* (Leicester, UK: Group for Large Local Authority Museums, 2000); Jocelyn Dodd and Richard Sandell, *Including Museums: Perspectives on Museums, Galleries and Social Inclusion* (Leicester, UK: Research Center for Museums and Galleries, 2001); and Richard Sandell, "Social Inclusion, the Museum and the Dynamics of Sectoral Change," *Museum and Society* 1, no. 1 (2003); (g) valuable suggestions by colleagues from various countries whose help and suggestions the author eagerly looked for; and other secondary sources. Obviously the sample is neither exhaustive nor "pure," as it

includes institutions that may not strictly speaking fall within the city museum category, simply because they are called "municipal." The need for a clear definition of what a city museum is and stands for is paramount.

The city museums that took part in this research form a very diverse body of institutions, of quite different background, institutional profile, size, type of collections, and work. These museums are

1–2) the Historical and Folk Museum of Larissa and the Historical and Folk Museum of Karditsa (Greece);

3) the City Museum of Barcelona (Spain);

4) the Historical Museum of Strasbourg (France);

5–6) the Historical Museum of Amsterdam and the City Museum of Zoetermeer (The Netherlands);

7) the City Museum of Luxembourg;

8) the Bruggemuseum (Belgium);

9–16) the Museum of Liverpool, the Discovery Museum in Newcastle, Lifetimes in Croydon, the Museum of London, Swansea Museum, the Ferens Art Gallery in Hull, the Stoke-on-Trent Pottery Museum, the First Garden City Heritage Museum in Hertfordshire (UK);

17–18) the Bohuslans Museum in Uddevala and the Skövde Museum (Sweden);

19) the Copenhagen City Museum (Denmark);

20) the Oslo City Museum (Norway);

21) the Helsinki City Museum (Finland);

22) the Historical Museum of Lausanne (Switzerland);

23–24) the City Museum of Cologne and the Municipal Museum of Munich (Germany);

25) the Nordico Museum (Austria);

26) the City Museum of Ljubljana (Slovenia);

27) the Budapest Historical Museum (Hungary);

28) the Historical Museum of Warsaw (Poland);

29) the Moscow City Museum (Russia);

30) the Lower East Side Tenement Museum, New York (United States);

31) the District Six Museum, Cape Town (South Africa);

32) the Addis Ababa Museum (Ethiopia);

33) the Hiratsuka City Museum (Japan);

34–35) the Susannah Place Museum and the Museum of Sydney (Australia).

16. In two cases (Bruggemuseum, Helsinki Museum) the museum is not housed in a single building, but operates through a network of buildings and satellite

museums, some of which are monumental landmarks of the city, covering more extensive urban and subterritories.

17. The scale of this funding differs among the museums in the sample and there are also some very interesting exceptions, mainly from Britain, Australia, and the United States. For instance, the Museum of Liverpool only partly relied on public funding (50 percent of its annual budget), the Museum of London relied on 60 percent, the Museum of Sydney 65 percent, and the Lower East Side Tenement Museum 26 percent, whereas 80 percent of the District Six Museum's funds come from private sources and entrepreneurial approaches raise the remaining 20 percent. Other European museums that do not rely totally on public funding are the City Museum of Barcelona (76 percent public funding) and the Bohuslans Museum in Sweden (63 percent).

18. Exceptions are the Museums at Croydon (Lifetimes) and Sydney, which rely heavily on loaned collections (by 70 percent and 50 percent accordingly).

19. For instance, the Museum of Liverpool has specific interpretation and conservation policies. As part of the National Museums Liverpool network it also implements acquisition and disposal, exhibition, learning and access, marketing, diversity, and equal opportunities policies, as well as community consultation strategies. The Museums at Swansea and Croydon, the Discovery Museum in Newcastle, and the Museum of London all have acquisition and disposal, display, access, and learning policies. The Museum of London also implements audience development and collections care policies, and the Discovery Museum has a cultural diversity policy in force.

20. For instance, an interesting contemporary collecting project has been the *800 Lives of the Museum of Liverpool*, in which the public was invited to donate a piece of oral history, an object, or a photograph that said something about their life in the city between 1945 and today. The museum's aim was to collect from as wide an audience as possible.

21. Oral history, in its full potential, is used by the following museums that participated in this survey project: the Historical Museum of Amsterdam, the City Museum of Zoetermeer, the Museum of Liverpool, Lifetimes in Croydon, the Museum of London, the Stoke-on-Trent Pottery Museum, the First Garden City Heritage Museum, the City Museum of Ljubljana, the Budapest History Museum,

Moscow City Museum, the Lower East Side Tenement Museum, the District Six Museum, the Susannah Place Museum, and the Hiratsuka City Museum.

22. Data provided by these museums: Helsinki, Swansea, Liverpool, London, Lifetimes (Croydon), Larissa, Discovery Museum, Stoke-on-Trent Pottery Museum, Ferens Art Gallery, Zoetermeer, Lower East Side Tenement Museum, District Six Museum.

23. Data provided by the Amsterdam Historical Museum and the Lower East Side Tenement Museum.

24. Data provided by these museums: Amsterdam, Zoetermeer, Lifetimes (Croydon), Liverpool, London, Swansea, Copenhagen, Warsaw, Moscow, Sydney, Stoke-on-Trent Pottery Museum, the Lower East Side Tenement Museum, the District Six Museum, the Addis Ababa Museum.

25. Data provided by these museums: Amsterdam, Helsinki, Cologne, Warsaw, the Bruggemuseum, the Discovery Museum, the Stoke-on-Trent Pottery Museum, the Lower East Side Tenement Museum, the District Six Museum, the Susannah Place Museum.

26. Such as those of the Lower East Side Tenement Museum, the Susannah Place Museum, Helsinki City Museum.

27. Examples provided by the museums of London, Warsaw, Moscow, and the Lower East Side Tenement Museum.

28. Data provided by the museums of Larissa, London, Skövde, Bohuslans, Copenhagen, Helsinki, Lausanne, Ljubljana, Sydney, Stoke-on-Trent Pottery Museum, Lower East Side Tenement Museum, District Six Museum.

29. Museums were asked to use Likert scale ratings, from 1 (fully disagree) to 9 (fully agree), to evaluate six predetermined statements. The most contentious ones have been "Self-representation by communities is a priority in our museum" and "A city museum must find out what the local community needs and adjust its work accordingly." Both sought to reveal the level of the museum's commitment toward community involvement and role in the planning and implementation of museum work. For these two, top ratings were provided by the Museum of Liverpool, Moscow City Museum, the Zoetermeer Museum (9, 9 respectively) and Stoke-on-Trent Museum (8, 9). Low ratings were given by the City Museum of

Luxembourg (1, 1), the City Museum of Barcelona (2, 4), the Warsaw Museum (3, 4), the Lower East Tenement Museum (4, 4), and the Amsterdam Historical Museum (4, 5). Especially for statement (c) low ratings (3 and 4) were also given by the Bruggemuseum, Copenhagen Museum, the Budapest Historical Museum, Helsinki Museum, and the Historical Museum of Lausanne.

30. The Museum of London and the Amsterdam Historical Museum are the main two paradigms of excellence, so voted by ten and six other museums respectively. Helsinki City Museum follows with three votes and then with two votes each the city museums of Basel, Luxembourg, Copenhagen, Zagreb, Malmö, Mölndals, Sunderland, and the Lower East Side Tenement Museum.

31. Interesting information on this matter was provided by the exhibition Global Cities, which was hosted in Tate Modern, London (20 June–27 August 2007); see www.tate.org.uk/modern/exhibitions/globalcities/default.shtm.

32. Three vision and mission statements were particularly forward looking; they are quoted here at length:

National Museums Liverpool, of which the Museum of Liverpool (due to reopen in a new building in 2010), is an integral part:
    Vision: We will be progressive and outward looking, exciting and inspiring people in ways that are inclusive and challenging.
    We believe that:
    NML has a responsibility to the whole of society. Everyone, regardless of age, identity, ability, or background, has a right to expect that we will be enjoyable and welcoming, providing routes to discovery, awareness, and learning for all.
    NML is committed to study, care for, and enhance our world-class collections, making them accessible to all.
    NML is a creative, energetic, and dynamic organization which must be managed imaginatively and effectively. We are prepared to identify and embrace opportunities, to experiment, take risks, and use innovative approaches to achieve our aims.
    NML must always be modern, radical, and responsive. We will build on our strengths, but we thrive on change. We believe in continuous assessment, transparency, and openness, listening and reacting to our users, and in improvement of all that we do.
    Teamwork and cooperation is valued and inherent in all that NML does. We will create a working environment where respect for different roles and talents is paramount, and all staff feel motivated, promoting quality, trust, and integrity.

NML grows stronger through partnerships—community, cultural, educational, and business. We will build such relationships wherever it helps us achieve our aims, while helping others achieve theirs.

City Museum of Zoetermeer:
The museum exists to preserve the (im)material heritage of the City of Zoetermeer. This means that the museum focuses on the history (or roots) and the identity of Zoetermeer for the benefit of the inhabitants of Zoetermeer, and secondly for the benefit of the (external) general public. In practice this means that the foundation is occupied with the conservation, preservation, gathering, and research of the collection, with its presentation and with the museological business task. Besides this the museum aims—as a living and lively house of the city—to be a platform, where discussions are started and where citizens of all sections of society work together with the museum on the museological/educational presentation of subjects, objects, and stories, which are close to the people and which refer to actual social topics.

The Museum of London, which provides a succinct statement of its mission:
The Museum of London's mission is to inspire a passion for London and to increase public understanding, appreciation, and awareness of London's cultural heritage, histories, and identities.
The core values are:
Engagement with diverse audiences and communities. We value engagement with diverse audiences and communities in ways that contribute to lifelong learning. Central to achieving this, we aim to challenge, excite, and involve our visitors, clients, and stakeholders.
Then stewardship:
We value the collections and research as central to our vision of understanding and presenting an ever-evolving knowledge about London's histories. The Museum of London Group is custodian of its collections for future generations.

BIBLIOGRAPHY

Anderson, David. *Reinventing the Museum.* Walnut Creek, CA: Rowman & Littlefield, 2004.

Archibald, R. Robert. *The New Town Square: Museums and Communities in Transition.* Walnut Creek, CA: AltaMira Press, 2004.

Black, Graham. *The Engaging Museum: Developing Museums for Visitor Involvement.* London: Routledge, 2005.

Dodd, Jocelyn, and Richard Sandell. *Including Museums: Perspectives on Museums, Galleries, and Social Inclusion.* Leicester, UK: Research Center for Museums and Galleries, 2001.

Hooper-Greenhill, Eilean, et al. *Museums and Social Inclusion: The GLLAM Report.* Leicester, UK: Group for Large Local Authority Museums, 2000.

Johnson, Nichola. "Discovering the City." *Museum International,* no. 187, vol. 47, no. 3 (July–September 1995): 4–6.

Jones, Ian. "A City Museum for the Twenty-First Century: Cardiff's Example." *En Volo* 22 (July–September, 2006): 24–29 (in Greek).

Kavanagh, Gaynor, and Elizabeth Frostick, eds. *Making City Histories in Museums.* Leicester: Leicester University Press, 1998.

Kirchberg, Volker. "Categorizing Urban Tasks: Functions of Museums in the Post-Industrial City." *Curator* 46, no. 1 (2003): 60–79.

Kistemaker, Renée, ed. *City Museums as Centers of Civic Dialogue? Proceedings of the Fourth Conference of the International Association of City Museums, Amsterdam, 3–5 November 2005.* Amsterdam: Amsterdam Historical Museum, 2006.

Lorente, Pedro, ed. *The Role of Museums and the Arts in the Urban Regeneration of Liverpool.* Leicester: Center for Urban History, University of Leicester, 1996.

Merriman, Nick. "The Peopling of London Project," in *Cultural Diversity: Redeveloping Museum Audiences in Britain,* edited by Eilean Hooper-Greenhill, 119–148. Leicester: Leicester University Press, 1997.

Mouliou, Marlen. "Mapping the 'World' of City Museums: Traces and Clues." *En Volo* 22 (July–September 2006): 8–17 (in Greek).

Museum International, no. 187, vol. 47, no. 3 (July–September 1995).

Museum International, no. 231, vol. 58, no. 3 (September 2006).

Parker, Sandra, et al. *Neighborhood Renewal and Social Inclusion: The Role of Museums, Archives, and Libraries.* London: Resource and University of Northumbria, 2002.

Stephens, Simon. "City Limits." *Museums Journal* 105, no. 10 (October 2005): 22–25.

Index

About the Contributors

Marie Louise Bourbeau (McGill University, 1979) enjoys a career in different styles of lyrical performance (Vienna State Opera Ensemble, Helios 18 Baroque Music, musical comedy, etc.). As vocal coach, she focuses on the embodiment of the voice as enabler of the self (Ateliers Body-Voice Dynamics). She is co-owner of master sharing international inc., where she collaborates in the research, conception, and implementation of projects and installations born at the conjuncture of the worlds of art and science.

Caroline Butler-Bowdon is head curator of the Museum of Sydney *on the site of first Government House*, a property of the Historic Houses Trust of New South Wales. Her recent publications include *Homes in the Sky: Apartment Living in Australia* (coauthor, 2007), *Sydney Then and Now* (2005), *Bridging Sydney* (contributing author, 2006), and *Talking about Sydney: Population, Community and Culture in Contemporary Sydney* (coeditor, 2006). She has also curated and cocurated numerous exhibitions at MOS, including Art Deco; Sydney at Federation: 1880–1910; and Leunig Animated. Her most recent exhibition was Homes in the Sky: Apartment Living in Sydney.

Szu-yun Chang is a senior researcher at the Department of Cultural Affairs of the Taipei City Government. She has been involved in various museum projects in Taiwan.

Chi-jung Chu is a PhD candidate at the London School of Economics and Political Science. Before joining LSE, she worked at the Taipei Fine Arts Museum and the Department of Cultural Affairs of the Taipei City Government. Her research interests cover museums, art, and comparative cultural policy studies.

Anja Dauschek has been head of the planning team for the City Museum of Stuttgart since 2007, being responsible for developing the city's first city museum. From 2000 to 2006 she worked as a museum consultant for LORD Cultural Resources, managing the company's Berlin office as a principal. She holds an MA in American Studies from the University of Munich and a PhD in European Ethnography from the University of Hamburg. In addition, she attended the Museum Studies Program at George Washington University, Washington, D.C. Currently she lectures in museum studies at the universities of Tübingen and Berlin.

Geoffrey Edwards (PhD, Laval University, 1987) is holder of one of Canada's Senior Research Chairs, in a domain called cognitive geomatics, and is director of the Laboratory for the Exploration of Media Immersion for Rehabilitation (EMIR). His research focus is currently oriented toward arts-enabled installations articulated around the body in space for both rehabilitation and museology, the exploration of issues of identity and difference, and the integration of virtual worlds into museum exhibits and other installations. Co-owner of master sharing international inc., he maintains a series of blogs and is active as both a scientist and an artist within the virtual world of Second Life.

Max Hebditch (CBE, MA, Hon D Litt, FSA, FMA) is chairman of the Taunton Cultural Consortium, which provides advice to local government on cultural development as part of the regeneration of the town center. The consortium represents museums, theater, music, and the visual arts, together with colleges, performing organizations, and the creative industries. He is a trustee of Lyme Regis Museum. He was director of the Museum of London from 1977 to 1997, and is a former president of the [United Kingdom] Museums Association (1990–1992) and chairman of the United Kingdom Committee of the International Council of Museums (ICOM; 1981–1987).

Susan Hunt has worked as a curator in various roles of historic site management, arts administration, and cultural programming with the Historic Houses Trust of New South Wales for over twenty years. From 2000 to 2005 she was head curator of the Museum of Sydney *on the site of first Government House.* During that time she curated many exhibitions, including Encountering India: Colonial Photography 1850–1911; Terre Napoléon: Australia through French Eyes; Lure of the Southern Seas: The Voyages of Dumont d'Urville 1826–1840; and Capetown: Half Way to Sydney. In 2006 she was appointed general manager, properties and is currently acting deputy director of the Historic Houses Trust.

Ian Jones has worked for the British Council in Finland and in Guyana on a project supported by the Inter-American Development Bank. He has been involved in museum projects in Poland; with Polish museologist Miroslaw Borusiewicz, he helped found the Polish Museum Center. He is a former university lecturer and has been a visiting lecturer at the Universities of Massie, New Zealand, and Pierre Mendès France in Grenoble, France. Currently, he is secretary of CAMOC (the Collections and Activities of Museums of Cities), one of the international committees of ICOM.

Jack Lohman is director of the Museum of London Group. He has worked for English Heritage, developing museums and exhibitions both nationally and internationally, and was the chief executive officer of Iziko Museums of Cape Town, an organization consisting of fifteen national museums. Jack Lohman is professor of museum design and communication at the Bergen National Academy of Arts in Norway, chair of the United Kingdom

Committee of ICOM, chair of the Advisory Committee of the Rothschild Foundation Europe, and a member of the UK National Commission of UNESCO. He is also a board member of Warsaw City Museum and editor-in-chief of UNESCO's publication series "Museums and Diversity."

Marlen Mouliou is an archaeologist and holds an MA and a PhD in Museum Studies from the University of Leicester (UK). Since 1997, she has worked for the Hellenic Ministry of Culture in the Directorate of Museums, Exhibitions, and Educational Programs. For the last seven years, she has also taught museology as an adjunct lecturer at the universities of Thessaly (Department of History, Archaeology, and Social Anthropology) and Athens (postgraduate museum studies program). Her research and published work is on issues of museum theory and practice, especially the philosophies and practices of archaeological and city museums. She is a founding member of the editorial board of the scientific journal *Tetradia Mouseiologias* (Museological Notebooks), which has been published annually since 2004 in Greek.

Gulchachak Rakhimzyanovna Nazipova is the director general of the National Museum of Tatarstan. She holds an MPhil and a PhD in history, and is a corresponding member of the Petrovsky Academy of Sciences and Arts and a member of the Board of ICOM Russia. She is the author of a number of books and booklets and more than sixty articles on the history of culture, issues about the development of museums past and present, and topical issues of museum life and culture.

Chet Orloff is director of the Pamplin Collection, adjunct professor of urban studies and planning at Portland State University, director emeritus (1991–2001) of the Oregon Historical Society, and founding president of the Museum of the City. He serves on numerous local, national, and international committees and commissions relating to history, museums, and planning. He practices history in Portland, Oregon, USA.

Georges Prévélakis has taught at the Sorbonne and at Sciences Po in Paris since 1984. He has also taught at John Hopkins University, Boston University, and, during two academic years, Tufts University, where he occupied the Constantine Karamanlis Chair in Hellenic and Southeastern European Studies (2003–2005). His research focuses on political and cultural geography theory, urban planning, diasporas, and European and eastern Mediterranean geopolitics. He is author of *Les Balkans, cultures et géopolitique* (1994, 1996, and 1999), *Les réseaux des diasporas* (1996), *Géopolitique de la Grèce* (1997, 2006), and *Athènes: urbanisme, culture et politique* (2000), as well as more than a hundred scientific articles. He is a member of many scientific and academic committees and institutions, including the Scientific Committee of the Museum of Europe in Brussels.

Eric Sandweiss is associate professor and Carmony Chair of History at Indiana University, where he also serves as editor of the *Indiana Magazine of History*. Prior to joining the university, he was director of research for the Missouri Historical Society in St. Louis.